I0108862

THE

AUGSBURG CONFESSION,

LITERALLY TRANSLATED FROM THE ORIGINAL LATIN
WITH THE MOST IMPORTANT ADDITIONS OF THE
GERMAN TEXT INCORPORATED:

TOGETHER WITH

THE GENERAL CREEDS;

AN INTRODUCTION AND NOTES

BY

CHARLES P. KRAUTH, D.D.,

NORTON PROFESSOR IN THE THEOLOGICAL SEMINARY
OF THE EVANGELICAL LUTHERAN CHURCH,
PHILADELPHIA

www.JustandSinner.com

AUGSBURG CONFESSION
LITERALLY TRANSLATED FROM THE
ORIGINAL LATIN WITH THE MOST
IMPORTANT ADDITIONS OF THE GERMAN
TEXT INCORPORATED

By CHARLES P. KRAUTH

Just & Sinner
425 East Lincoln Ave.
Watseka, IL 60970

www.JustandSinner.com

ISBN 10: 0692465766
ISBN 13: 978-0692465769

TABLE OF CONTENTS

ADVERTISEMENT

FOR the edification of its members in the Doctrines of our Church, and to have within reach of all a complete and approved edition, in English, of the great Augsburg Confession,—the fundamental Confession of Protestant Christianity,—*The Tract and Book Society* of St. John's Evangelical Lutheran Church, of this city, two years ago, entered into arrangements to have this desideratum supplied. The book has been delayed beyond anticipation. The Board of Managers regret that they have been unable to present it sooner; but they congratulate the members of the Society, and the Church at large, that, in the good Providence of God, they now have it in their power to deliver an English edition of our Confession, at once complete in itself, and accompanied with an Introduction and Notes, which will doubtless be appreciated according to their exalted worth. Numerous have been the issues of our Society during the many years of its existence, but none of them are at all to be compared with this, in the importance of the place which it is to fill, or in the labor, scholarly care, and valuable learning which have been bestowed upon it. May the Lord bless it to the good of all into whose hands it may come!

A lasting debt of gratitude is due to Dr. C. P. Krauth for the very able manner in which he has prepared what is herewith respectfully submitted by

THE BOARD OF MANAGERS.

PHILADELPHIA, April, 1868.

INTRODUCTION

1. THE NATURE AND NECESSITY OF CREEDS

THE Holy Scriptures are a perfect rule of faith. Because they are such they beget a true faith in the heart which receives them aright. The faith, thus begotten, instinctively expresses itself in words. Those words, whether simply thought in the mind, uttered with the lips, written by our own hand, or assented to when written by another, are a Creed. A Christian Creed is simply the human expression, oral or mental, of the faith which has been received from God's Word. When, indeed, there can be and is no dispute whatever, on the part of any one, as to the meaning of God's Word, its own language is the most perfect mode of expressing our faith. Then, and then only, is it true that the Bible is our Creed. But when there can be and is a dispute as to the meaning of certain words in it, we can no longer express our Creed or Confession in its words, because, as the object of a public Confession is to testify to others what we hold, and the very words we use are understood in more senses than one, we do not really confess or testify by using them—as some will understand them in one sense, and others in another. In this case we conceal our faith, instead of making it known. When God uses words to express His mind, they are a rule of faith because His meaning is absolute truth. When we use these same words to express our mind they are but a Creed, for we use them as we understand them, and that understanding may be incorrect. When He uses them the question is, What does He mean? and what He means, is the rule of faith. When we use them the question is, What do we mean? and what we mean, is our Confession of faith. As a rule of faith the Word of God is absolute truth, but the meaning intended in the use of those very same words, by an errorist, may be false. When our Lord, for instance, says the wicked shall "go away into everlasting punishment," his words are a rule of faith, and bind us to believe that there shall be literally no end to the misery of the wicked; but when a Universalist uses these same words as his Creed, they mean the very reverse of what the Savior meant; their sense, as a Universalist Creed, is exactly the opposite of their sense as a divine rule of faith, and so used they cease to mean the truth.

2. EARLY CREEDS

Not, therefore, as opposed to the supreme authority of the Word of God, but as the result of recognizing it, not to set up the opinions of man against divine truth, but to prevent their being thus set up, to show that she has taken to her inmost heart the faith set forth in the Holy Scriptures, the Church, from the beginning, has had Creeds, or statements of faith. The oldest and most universally received of these is the APOSTLES' CREED, so called, not because it was written by them, but because it is a summary of their teachings. Our blessed Lord himself gave the germ of the Apostles' Creed, both as to its substance and its form, when He ordained his Apostles to go into all the world, and to make disciples of all nations, by baptizing them into the name of the Father, Son, and Holy Ghost, teaching them to observe all things whatsoever he had commanded them. Next to the Apostles' is the NICENE CREED, so called from the place at which the General Council met at which it was set forth. The third General Confession is the ATHANASIAN CREED, which, though not the work of Athanasius, correctly exhibits the great doctrines which he so earnestly maintained. These three Creeds the Lutheran Church accepts as her own, and by them testifies to her historical unity with the Ancient Church.

3. ROMAN CATHOLICISM AND ITS CREED

An age of darkness is a creedless age; corruption in doctrine works best when it is unfettered by an explicit statement of that doctrine. Between the Athanasian Creed (probably about A.D. 434) and the sixteenth century, there is no new General Creed. Error loves ambiguities. In the contest with Rome the Reformers complained bitterly that she refused to make an explicit official statement of her doctrine. "Our opponents," says the Apology, "do not bestow the labor, that there may be among the people some certain statement of the chief points of the ecclesiastical doctrines."

Just in proportion to the blind devotion of men to Popery were they reluctant to have its doctrines stated in an authorized form, and only under the compulsion of a public sentiment which was wrought by the Reformation, did the Church of Rome at length convene the Council of Trent. Its decisions were not completed and set forth until seventeen years after Luther's death, and thirty-three years after the Augsburg Confession. The proper date of the distinctive life of a particular Church is furnished by her Creed. Tested by the General Creeds, the Evangelical Lutheran Church has the same claim as the Roman Church to be considered in unity with the early Church,—but as a particular Church, with a distinctive bond and token of doctrinal union, she is more than thirty years older than the Roman Church. Our Church has the oldest distinctive Creed now in use in any large division of Christendom. That Creed is the Confession of Augsburg. Could the Church have set forth and maintained such a Confession as that of Augsburg before the time over which the Dark Ages extended, those Dark Ages could not have come. There would have been no Reformation, for none would have been needed.

4. THE AUGSBURG CONFESSION: PRELIMINARIES TO PREPARATION OF

The mighty agitations caused by the restoration of divine truth by Luther and his great co-workers, had led to attempts at harmonizing the conflicting elements, especially by action at the Diets of the Empire. At the Diet of Worms (1521)

Luther refuses to retract, and the Edict goes forth commanding his seizure and the burning of his books; at the Diet of Nuremberg (1522) Cheregati, the Papal Nuncio, demands the fulfilment of the Edict of Worms, and the assistance of all faithful friends of the Church against Luther. The first Diet at Spires (1526) had virtually annulled the Edict of Worms, by leaving its execution to the unforced action of the different Estates, and it promised the speedy convocation of a General Council, or at least of a National Assembly. The second Diet at Spires (1529) quenched the hopes inspired by this earlier action. It decreed that the Edict of Worms should be strictly enforced where it had already been received; the celebration of the Roman Mass protected, and the preachers bound to confine themselves to the doctrine of the Roman Church in their teachings. The Protest of the Evangelical Princes against this decision, originated the name PROTESTANTS.

The Protestant Princes made their appeal to a free General Council. Charles V, after vainly endeavoring to obtain the consent of the Pope to the convocation of a General Council, summoned the Diet at Augsburg, promising to appear in person, and to give a gracious hearing to the whole question, so that the "one only Christian truth might be maintained, that all might be subjects and soldiers of the one Christ, and live in the fellowship and unity of one Church." To this end the Emperor directed the friends of the Evangelical faith to prepare for presentation to the Diet, a statement on the points of division.

In consequence of this order of the Emperor, the Elector of Saxony, who was the leader of the Evangelical Princes, directed Luther, in conjunction with the other theologians at Wittenberg, to draw up a summary of doctrine, and a statement of the abuses to be corrected. The statement drawn up in consequence of this, had, as its groundwork, Articles which were already prepared; and as the Augsburg Confession is the ripest result of a series of labors, in which this was one, and as much confusion of statement exists on the relations of these labors, it may be useful to give the main points in chronological order.

1. 1529. October 1, 2, 3. The Conference at Marburg took place between Luther and the Saxon divines upon the one side, and Zwingli and the Swiss divines on the other. Luther, in conjunction with others of our great theologians, prepared the XV Marburg Articles, October, 1529. These Articles were meant to show on what points the Lutherans and Zwinglians agreed, and also to state the point on which they did not agree, and as a fair statement of the points, disputed and undisputed, were signed by all the theologians of both parties.

2. 1529. Oct. 16. On the basis of these XV Articles were prepared, by Luther, with the advice and assistance of the other theologians, the XXII Articles of Schwabach, so called from the place at which they were presented.

3. 1529. Nov. 29. From the presentation of these XXII Articles at Smalcald, they are sometimes called the Smalcald Articles.

4. 1530. March 20. These XVII Articles of Luther revised were sent to Torgau, and were long

called the Torgau Articles, though they are in fact the revised Articles of Schwabach. These Articles are mainly doctrinal.

5. March 20. In addition to these, a special writing, of which Luther was the chief author, in conjunction with Melanchthon, Ionas, and Bugenhagen, was prepared by direction of the Elector, and sent to Torgau. These articles are on the abuses, and are the *Torgau Articles proper.*

6. The XVII doctrinal articles of Schwabach *formed the basis* of the doctrinal articles of the Augsburg Confession; the Articles of Torgau are the basis of its articles on abuses, and both these are mainly from the hand of Luther.

In six instances, the very numbers of the Schwabach Articles correspond with those of the Augsburg Confession. They coincide throughout, not only in doctrine, but in a vast number of cases word for word, the Augsburg Confession being a mere transcript, in these cases, of the Schwabach Articles. The differences are either merely stylistic, or are made necessary by the larger object and compass of the Augsburg Confession; but so thoroughly do the Schwabach Articles condition and shape every part of it, as to give it even the peculiarity of phraseology characteristic of Luther.

5. ITS AUTHORSHIP: LUTHER'S RELATIONS TO

To a large extent, therefore, Melanchthon's work is but an elaboration of Luther's, and to a large extent it is not an elaboration, but a reproduction. To Luther belong the doctrinal power of the Confession, its inmost life and spirit, and to Melanchthon its matchless form. Both are in some sense its authors, but the most essential elements of it are due to Luther, who is by preeminence its author, as Melanchthon is its composer. If the authorship of the Confession should be claimed for Melanchthon to the exclusion of Luther, it would open the second great Reformer to the charge of the most unscrupulous plagiarism. Even had Luther, however, had no direct share in the Augsburg Confession, the assertion would be too sweeping that he was in *no sense* its author. Great leading minds are in some sense the authors of all works that have germinated directly from their thoughts. But Luther was, in a peculiar sense, the author of Melanchthon's theological life; he was, as Melanchthon loved to call him, "his most dear father." All the earliest and purest theology of Melanchthon is largely but a repetition, in his own graceful way, of Luther's thoughts; and the Augsburg Confession is in its inmost texture the theology of the New Testament as Luther believed it.

6. ABSENCE OF LUTHER FROM AUGSBURG

For the absence of Luther from Augsburg, the reasons constantly assigned in history are obviously the real ones. Luther was not only under the Papal excommunication, but he was an outlaw under the imperial ban. In the rescript of the Emperor he was styled "the evil fiend in human form," "the fool," and "the blasphemer." His person would have been legally subject to seizure. The

Diet at Spires (1529) had repeated the Decree of Worms. The Elector would have looked like a plotter of treason had Luther been thrust by him before the Emperor, and with the intense hatred cherished by the Papistical party toward Luther, he would not have been permitted to leave Augsburg alive. The Elector was so thoroughly anxious to have Luther with him, that at first he allowed his wishes to obscure his judgment,—he attached such importance to the mild language of Charles V, that he allowed himself to hope, yet, as his letter of March 14th shows, rather feebly, that even Luther might be permitted to appear. Luther left Wittenberg on the assumption that he perhaps might be permitted to come to Augsburg. But a safe conduct was denied him. Had it been desired by the Elector to have Luther out of the way, it would have been far easier to the Elector, and pleasanter to Luther, to have kept him at Wittenberg.

That Luther came to Coburg, is proof of the ardent desire to have his counsel and co-operation; that he stopped there, shows the greatness of the peril that would have attended his going further. But Luther's safety was not merely provided for by his detention here, but by placing him in the old castle of the Duke of Coburg, which occupies a commanding height, more than five hundred feet above the town, and which is so well fortified by nature and art, that during the Thirty Years' War, Wallenstein besieged it in vain.

The awful loneliness of such a spot would have impressed the soul of Luther under any circumstances, but the isolation of the place seems to have been meant to give him additional security. The arrangements were planned by loving friends for his safety. Luther perfectly understood the character and object of the arrangements, before they were made, while they were in progress, and after all was over. Thus, April 2d, writing before his journey, he says: "I am going with the Prince, *as far as Coburg*, and Melanchthon and Jonas with us, until it is known what will be attempted at Augsburg." In another letter of same date: "I am not summoned to go to Augsburg, but for certain reasons, I only accompany the Prince on his journey through his own dominions." June 1, he writes: "I am waiting on the borders of Saxony, midway between Wittenberg and Augsburg, for it was not *safe* to take me to Augsburg."

The expressions of impatience which we find in his letters during his stay at Coburg, only show that in the ardor of his great soul, in moments of intense excitement, the reasons for his detention at the castle, which commended themselves to his cooler judgment, seemed reasons no longer—death seemed nothing—he would gladly face it as he had faced it before, only to be in body where he was already in heart. "I burn," he says, "to come, though uncommanded and uninvited." His seeming impatience, his agony, his desire to hear often, his refusal for the moment to listen to any excuses, were all inevitable with such a spirit as Luther's under the circumstances; yet for places four days' journey apart, in those troublous times, of imperfect communication, with special couriers carrying all the letters, there was an extraordinary amount of correspondence. We have about seventy letters of Luther written to Augsburg during the Diet, and we know of thirty-two written by Melanchthon to Luther, and of thirty-nine written by Luther to Melanchthon in the five months of correspondence, during the Diet, or connected with it in the time preceding.

7. CORRESPONDENCE WITH LUTHER

MELANCHTHON'S LETTERS OF MAY 4TH

Luther and Melanchthon went in company to Coburg, and at Coburg the "Exordium" of the Confession was written. At Augsburg, Melanchthon, as was his wont, elaborated it to a yet higher finish. May 4, he writes to Luther: "I have made the exordium of our Apology" (that is, the Confession) "somewhat more finished in style (retorikoteron), than I wrote it at Coburg." Speaking of his work he says: "In a short time, *I myself will bring it*, or if the Prince will not permit me to come, *I will send it.*"

By the Apology or Defense is meant the Confession, which was originally designed to be in the main a defense of the Evangelical (Lutheran) Confessors, especially in regard to their practical application of their principles in the correction of abuses. The second part was the one which at the time of the preparation of the Confession was regarded as the more difficult, and for the immediate objects contemplated, the more important. The articles of faith were designed as a preparation for the second part, and the judgment of Forstemann and others that by the "Exordium,"

Melanchthon meant not the Preface, which there seems to be evidence was written in German by Bruck, and translated into Latin by Jonas, "but the whole first part of the Confession, is not without much to render it probable."

If we take Melanchthon's language, in his letter of May 5, grammatically, it seems to settle it, that the Exordium was the whole first part, for it is inconceivable that he would desire to come all the way to Coburg to show Luther merely the Preface, more especially as we know that the Confession itself was nearly finished at the time. In a letter of the same date (May 4th), to Viet Dietrich, who was with Luther, he says: "I will shortly run over to you, that I may bring to the Doctor (Luther), the Apology which is to be offered to the Emperor, that he (Luther) may examine it."

THE ELECTOR'S LETTERS OF MAY 11TH

For very obvious reasons, Melanchthon could not be spared from Augsburg at this time even for an hour, to say nothing of the hazards which might have been incurred by the journey, which his great anxiety for a personal conference with Luther inclined him to make. But on May 11th, the Elector sent to Luther the Confession, with a letter, in which he speaks of it as meant to be a careful revision of those very articles of which Luther was the main author. He says to Luther (Augsburg, May 11th): "As you and our other theologians at Wittenberg, have brought into summary statement the articles of religion about which there is dispute, it is our wish to let you know that

Melanchthon has further revised the same, and reduced them to a *form*, which we hereby send you." "And it is our desire that you would further revise the same, *and give them a thorough examination*, and at the *same time* (daneben) you would also write how you like it, or what you think proper to add about it or to it, and in order that, on his Majesty's arrival, which is looked for in a short time, we may be ready, send back the same carefully secured and sealed, without delay, to this place, by the letter-carrier who takes this."

Luther had been the chief laborer in the articles of which the Elector declared the Confession to be but a revision and reducing to shape—there could be little room for large changes, and as the Emperor was expected speedily, the time was too pressing to allow of elaborate discussions, which were indeed unneeded where all were so absolute a unit in faith as our Confessors were. That margin would have been narrow, and that time short, indeed, on which and in which Luther could not have written enough to kill any Confession which tampered with the truth.

The Elector's whole letter expressly assigns the natural and cogent reason, that Luther's judgment might be needed at once, in consequence of the expected advent of the Emperor, a point which Melanchthon's letter of the same date also urges. The haste is evidence of the anxiety to have Luther's opinion and approval, as a *sine qua non.*

The Diet had been summoned for April 8th. It was soon after postponed to the 1st of May, and at this later date, had it not been for the delay of the Emperor in appearing, the articles of Luther, on which the Confession was afterwards based, would themselves have been offered. As it was, it was needful to be ready at any hour for the approach of Charles. The letter of the Elector seems to imply that the original of the Confession was sent to Luther. Great care was taken to prevent copies from being multiplied, as the enemies were eager to see it. Even on June 25th, the day of its presentation, the Latin Confession, in Melanchthon's own handwriting, was given to the Emperor.

MELANCHTHON'S LETTER OF MAY 11TH

With this letter of the Elector was sent a letter from Melanchthon addressed "to Martin Luther, his most dear father." In it he says: "Our Apology is sent to you, although it is more properly a Confession, for the Emperor will have no time for protracted discussion. Nevertheless, I have said those things which I thought most profitable or fitting. With this design I have embraced nearly all the articles of faith, for Eck has put forth the most diabolical slanders against us, to which I wished to oppose a remedy. I request you, in accordance with your own spirit, to decide concerning the whole writing (*Pro tuo spiritu de toto scripto statues*). A question is *referred to you*, to which I greatly desire an answer from you. What if the Emperor ... should prohibit our ministers from preaching at Augsburg? I have answered that we should yield to the wish of the Emperor, in whose city we are guests. But our old man is difficult to soften." (The "old man" is either the Elector John, so called to distinguish him from his son, John Frederick, or the old Chancellor Bruck.) "Whatever therefore you think, I beg that you will write it *in German on separate paper.*"

What Luther was to write was his judgment both as to the Confession and the question about preaching, and the "separate paper," on which he was particularly requested to write, must mean separate from that which held the Confession. One probable reason why Luther was so particularly requested not, as was very much his wont, to write upon the margin, was, that this original draft of the Confession might have been needed for presentation to the Emperor. The original of Luther's replies to the Elector on both points (for to the Elector and not to Melanchthon they were to be made, and were made), still remains. Both are together—neither is on the margin of anything, but both are written just as Melanchthon specially requested, "in German," and on "separate paper." It shows the most intense desire to have the assurance doubly sure of Luther's concurrence, that under all the pressure of haste, the original of the Confession was sent him.

That the highest importance was attached to Luther's judgment on this form of the Confession, is furthermore proved by the fact that after the Confession was dispatched (May 11), *everything was suspended at Augsburg*, till he should be heard from. "On the 16th of May, the Elector indicated to the other States, *that the Confession* was ready, but was not entirely closed up, but had been sent to Luther for examination." Shortly after Luther's reply of May 15, heartily indorsing the Confession, without the change of a word, was received at Augsburg.

It is called "*form* of Confession," in the Elector's letter to Luther, because the *matter* of the Confession had been prepared by Luther himself. Melanchthon's work was but to revise that matter, and give it "form," which revised form was to be subjected to the examination of all the Lutheran authorities and divines at Augsburg, and especially to Luther.

As to the articles of faith, and the abuses to be corrected, the matter of the Confession was already finished and furnished—much of it direct from Luther's hand, and all of it with his co-operation and approval. It was only as to the "form," the selection among various abuses, the greater or less amplitude of treatment, that all the questions lay. The "form of Confession" sent on May 11th was the Augsburg Confession, substantially identical with it as a whole, and, in all that is really essential to it, verbally identical. We have copies of it so nearly at the stage at which it then was as to know that this is the case. Melanchthon's letter expressly declares that nearly all the articles of faith had been treated, and the Augsburg Confession, in its most finished shape, only professes to give "about the sum of the doctrines held by us."

But we need not rest in inferences, however strong, in regard to this matter. We have direct evidence from Melanchthon himself, which will be produced, that Luther did decide, before its presentation, upon what, in Melanchthon's judgment, was the Augsburg Confession itself. His words prove that the changes which Luther did not see were purely those of niceties of style, or of a more ample elaboration of a very few points, mainly on the abuses; in fact, that Luther's approval had been given to the Confession, and that without it the Confession never would have been presented.

The Elector's letter of May 11th was answered by Luther, who heartily indorsed the Confession sent him, without the change of a word. Nothing was taken out, nothing was added, nothing was altered. He speaks admiringly, not reprovingly, of the moderation of its style, and confesses that it had a gentleness of manner of which he was not master.

As the Emperor still lingered, Melanchthon used the time to improve, here and there, the external form of the Confession. He loved the most exquisite accuracy and delicacy of phrase, and never ceased filing on his work. What topics should be handled under the head of abuses, was in the main perfectly understood, and agreed upon between him and Luther. The draft of the discussion of them was largely from Luther's hand, and all of it was indorsed by him.

The main matters were entirely settled, the principles were fixed, and the questions which arose were those of style, of selection of topics, of the mode of treating them, or of expediency, in which the faith was not involved. In regard to this, Luther speedily hears again from his son in the Gospel.

MELANCHTHON'S LETTER OF MAY 22

May 22d, Melanchthon wrote to Luther: "In the Apology, we daily change many things; the article on Vows, as it was more meagre than it should be, I have removed, and supplied its place with a discussion a little more full, on the same point. I am now treating of the power of the keys also. I wish you would run over the Articles of Faith; if you think there is no defect in them, we will treat of the other points as we best may (*utcunque*). For they are to be changed from time to time, and adapted to the circumstances." In the same letter he begs Luther to write to George, Duke of Saxony, because his letter would carry decisive weight with him: "there is need of your letters."

This letter shows:

1. That Melanchthon desired Luther to know all that he was doing.

2. That the Articles of Faith were finished, and that the changes were confined to the Articles on Abuses.

3. That in the discussions on Abuses, there were many questions which would have to be decided as the occasions, in the providence of God, would determine them.

From three to four days seems to have been the ordinary time of the letter-carrier between Augsburg and Coburg. The Elector sent the Confession May 11th; Luther replied May 15th, probably the very day he received it; his reply probably reached Augsburg May 20th, and two days after, Melanchthon sends him the Articles of Faith, with the elaboration which had taken place in the interval, and informs him of what he had been doing, and designs to do.

In part, on the assumption that Luther was not permitted to receive this letter, a theory was built by Rückert, a Rationalistic writer of Germany, that the Augsburg Confession was meant to be a compromise with Rome, and that it was feared that if Luther were not kept in the dark he would spoil the scheme. But even if Luther did not receive Melanchthon's letter and the Articles of May 22d, we deny that the rational solution would be that they were fraudulently held back by the friends of the Confession at Augsburg. Grant that Luther never received them. What then? The retention of them would have been an act of flagrant immorality; it was needless, and foolish, and hazardous; it is in conflict with the personal character of the great princes and leaders, political and theological, who were as little disposed as Luther, to compromise any principle with Rome. The Elector and Brück were on some points less disposed to be yielding than Luther. The theory is contradicted by the great body of facts, which show that Luther, though absent in body, was the controlling spirit at Augsburg. It is contradicted by the Confession itself, which is a presentation, calm in manner, but mighty in the matter, in which it overthrows Popery from the very foundation. It is contradicted by the fierce replies of the Papists in the Council, by the savage assaults of Popery upon it through all time, by the decrees of the Council of Trent, whose main polemical reference is to it. It is contradicted by the enthusiastic admiration which Luther felt, and expressed again and again, for the Confession.

The millions of our purified churches have justly regarded it for ages as the great bulwark against Rome, and the judgment of the whole Protestant world has been a unit as to its fundamentally Evangelical and Scriptural character over against Rome. Its greatest defenders have been the most able assailants of Popery.

It might as well be assumed that the Bible is a compromise with the Devil, and that the Holy Ghost was excluded from aiding in its production, lest he should embarrass the proceedings, as that the Augsburg Confession is, or was meant to be, a compromise with Popery, and that Luther was consequently prevented from having a share in producing it.

If the letter really never reached Luther, the theory that it was fraudulently kept at Augsburg by the friends of the Confession, that the whole thing was one of the meanest, and at the same time, most useless crimes ever committed, is so extreme, involves such base wickedness on the part of its perpetrators, that nothing but the strongest evidence or the most overwhelming presumptions justify a man in thinking such an explanation possible.

If this letter, or others, never reached Luther, it is to be attributed either to the imperfect mode of transmission, in which letters were lost, miscarried or destroyed by careless or fraudulent carriers, of which bitter complaints constantly occur in the letters of Luther and others at that time, or if there were any steps taken to prevent Luther's letters reaching him, these steps would be taken by the Romanists, who were now gathering in increasing force at Augsburg. The difficulty in the way of communicating with Luther increased, as his being at Coburg was kept secret from his enemies, and at his request, in a letter which we shall quote, was kept secret in June even from the body of his friends.

So much for the theory, granting its fact for argument's sake.

But the fact is that Luther did receive Melanchthon's letter of the 22d. The letter was not lost, but appears in all the editions of Melanchthon's letters, entire, and in the earliest histories of the Augsburg Confession, without a hint, from the beginning up to Rückert's time, that it had not been received. When we turn to Luther's letters, complaining of the silence of his friends, we find no evidence that Melanchthon's letter had not been received. They create, on the contrary, the strongest presumption that it had been received. As it was sent at once (Melanchthon says that he had hired a letter-carrier before he began the letter), it would reach Luther about May 25th.

Luther's letter of June 1st to Jacob Probst, in Bremen, shows that he had intelligence of the most recent date from Augsburg, that he was sharing in the cares and responsibilities of what was then passing: "Here, also, I am occupied with business for God, and the burden of the whole empire rests upon us." He then uses, in part, the very language of Melanchthon's letter of May 22d, as to the time when the Emperor would be at Augsburg. He quotes from that letter Melanchthon's very words in regard to Mercurinus: "He would have nothing *to* do with violent councils—that it had appeared at

Worms what violent councils would do. He desired the affairs of the Church to be peacefully arranged." He closes his account of things at Augsburg by saying: "You have an account of matters now as they *are to-day* at Augsburg" (*hodie habet*).

Luther did receive Melanchthon's letter of the 22d, and on June 1st quotes largely from it.

Up to this time, too, there is no complaint of suspension of communication with Augsburg, but, on the contrary, he reports up to the day on which he writes.

On June 2d Luther writes to Melanchthon. There is no word of complaint in this letter of any silence on the part of Melanchthon, or of others at Augsburg. He complains that he is so overrun with visitors as to be compelled to leave Coburg for a day, to create the impression that he is no longer there. "I beg of you, and the others with you, in future to speak and *write* so that *no one* will seek me here any longer; *for I wish to remain concealed*, and to have you, at the same time, to keep concealed, both in your words *and letters*." He then speaks of the report that the Emperor would not come to Augsburg at all, and of his deep anxiety. This letter shows what was the subject of Luther's intense anxiety on the following days. A thousand alarming rumors reached him, and he was anxious to hear, by every possible opportunity, from Augsburg; at the same time, wishing to be concealed, he had requested Melanchthon and his other friends to avoid sending letters in a way that would make it known that he was at Coburg. These two facts help to solve Luther's great solicitude to hear news, and also, in part, as we have said, to account for the irregularity in his receiving letters, as they would, in accordance with his direction of June 2d, be sent with secrecy. In Luther's letter of June 5th, he complains not that there had been a long delay, but that they did not write by every opportunity. These were sometimes quite frequent. In some cases more than one opportunity occurred in a day. None of Luther's anxiety is about the Confession. In Luther's letter to Melanchthon, of June 7th, he complains of the silence of his friends at Augsburg, but in a *playful tone.* In his letter of June 19th, to Cordatus, he says: "We have no *news* from Augsburg. Our friends at Augsburg write us none." In his letter to Gabriel Zwilling, June 19th, he says: "You will, perhaps, get the *news* from Bernhard, for our friends have not answered our letters through the whole month" (June). Luther's letter of *June 20th*, to Justus Jonas, gives direct evidence how long the interruption of correspondence continued: "Your letters have come at last, my Jonas, after we were well fretted for *three whole weeks* with your silence." The period, therefore, does not embrace May 22d, but only the first three weeks in June. There is no reason whatever, therefore, for doubting that Luther received Melanchthon's letter, and the Articles of Faith of May 22d. On June 1st, the Elector, John, sent Luther secret advices of an important proposition which he had received from the Emperor. If, therefore, there were any furtive and dishonorable course pursued toward Luther, the causes and results of it must, in some special manner, be found between the Elector's secret advices of June 1st and the letter to Luther from Augsburg, June 15th; but there is nothing in the course of events to suggest any such reason, even if there were a fact which seemed to require something of the sort—but there is no such fact. On the contrary, we shall produce a fact which will sweep away all necessity for any further discussion of this point.

We have seen, 1st, that the Confession was sent by the Elector, May 11th, to Luther, at Coburg, for his written judgment upon it, in its *first form.*

2d. That it was sent again, on the 22d of the same month, by Melanchthon, and was received by Luther, in its *second form.*

3d. We shall now show that it was sent as nearly as possible in its complete shape to Luther, for a *third time*, before it was delivered, and was approved by him in what may probably be called its *final form.*

The evidence to which we shall appeal is that of Melanchthon himself. It is first found in the Preface to his Body of Christian Doctrine (*Corpus Doctrinæ*), 1560, and also in the Preface to the first volume of the Wittenberg edition of his works in folio. It is reprinted in the Corpus Reformatorum, vol. ix, No. 6932. He there says, in giving a history of the Augsburg Confession:

I. "I brought together the principal points of the Confession, embracing pretty nearly the sum of the doctrine of our Churches."

II. "I assumed nothing to myself, for in the presence of the Princes and other officials, and of the preachers, it was discussed and determined upon in regular course, sentence by sentence."

III. "The complete form of the Confession was *subsequently (deinde)* sent to Luther, who wrote to the Princes that he had read the Confession and approved it. That these things were so done, the Princes, and other honest and learned men, *yet living*, well remember."

IV. "*After this (postea)*, before the Emperor Charles, in a great assemblage of the Princes, this Confession was read."

This extract shows, 1, that this complete Confession—the *tota forma*—the Articles on Doctrines and Abuses, as contrasted with any earlier and imperfect form of the Confession, was submitted to Luther.

2. This is wholly distinct from Luther's indorsement of the Confession as sent May 11th, for that was not the "*tota forma*," but relatively unfinished; that had not been discussed before Princes, officials, and preachers, for they were not yet at Augsburg. Nor was it then meant that the Confession should be made in the name of all the Evangelical States. It was to be limited to Saxony. Luther's reply to the letter of May 11th was not to the Princes, but to John alone. Up to May 11th, the Elector (with his suite) was the only one of the Princes at Augsburg. On the 12th, the Landgrave of Hesse came; on the 15th the Nurembergers. Not until after May 22d did that conference and discussion take place, of which Melanchthon speaks. After the whole form of the Confession had been decided upon, it was sent to Luther, received his final indorsement, and was presented to Charles. This complete form was identical in matter with the Confession as exhibited, although

verbal changes were made by Melanchthon up to
the very time of its delivery.

8. LUTHER'S OPINION OF THE AUGSBURG CONFESSION

On this point, we propose to let Luther speak
for himself.

1. 1530, May 15. In Luther's reply to the
Elector, he says: "I have read the Apology
(Confession), of Philip, from beginning to end; it
pleases me exceedingly well, and I know of
nothing by which I could better it, or change it, nor
would I be fitted to do it, for I cannot move so
moderately and gently. May Christ our Lord help,
that it may bring forth much and great fruit, as we
hope and pray. Amen."

These words of admiration for Melanchthon's
great gifts, came from Luther's inmost heart. Less
than six months before he had written to Jonas:
"All the Jeromes, Hillarys, and Macariuses
together, are not worthy to unloose the thong of
Philip's sandal. What have the whole of them
together done which can be compared with one
year of Philip's teaching, or to his one book of
Common Places?" Had Luther been at Augsburg,
he would have allowed the work of finishing "the
form of the Confession" to be given to no other
hands than Melanchthon's: "I prefer," he says,
"Melanchthon's books to my own, and would
rather have them circulated than mine. I was born
to battle with conspirators and devils, therefore my
books are more vehement and warlike. It is my
work to tear up the stumps and dead roots, to cut

away the thorns, to fill up the marshes. I am the rough forester and pioneer. But Melanchthon moves gently and calmly along, with his rich gifts from God's own hand, building and planting, sowing and watering."

2. Between June 8th and 25th, we have Melanchthon's declaration, cited in our former article, as to Luther's approval of the Confession in the form it took after the discussion.

3. June 3d. Luther to Melanchthon: "I yesterday reread your Apology entire, with care (*diligenter*), and it pleases me exceedingly."

4. July 6th, to Hausman: he speaks lovingly of "*our* Confession which our Philip hath prepared."

5. July 6, to Cordatus: "The Confession of ours was read before the whole empire. I am glad exceedingly to have lived to this hour, in which Christ through his so great Confessors, in so great an Assembly, has been preached in so glorious a Confession, and that word has been fulfilled: 'I will speak of thy testimonies in the presence of kings,' and this also has been fulfilled: 'and shall not be ashamed,' for 'him who confesses me before men' (it is the word of him who cannot lie), 'I also will confess before my Father who is in heaven.' "

6. July 6, to the Cardinal Albert, Archbishop of Mentz, Primate of Germany: "Your Highness, as well as the other orders of the empire, has doubtless read the Confession, delivered by ours, which I am persuaded is so composed, that with joyous lips, it may say with Christ: 'If I have spoken evil, bear witness of the evil; but if well, why smitest thou me?' It shuns not the light, and can sing with the Psalmist: 'I will speak of thy

testimonies before kings, and will not be ashamed.'
But I can well conceive that our adversaries will by
no means accept the doctrine, but much less are
they able to confute it. I have no hope whatever
that we can agree in doctrine; for their cause
cannot bear the light. Such is their bitterness, with
such hatred are they kindled, that they would
endure hell itself rather than yield to us, and
relinquish their new wisdom. I know that this our
doctrine is true, and grounded in the holy
Scriptures. By this Confession we clearly testify
and demonstrate that we have not taught wrongly
or falsely."

7. July 9, to Duke John, Elector of Saxony: "Our
adversaries thought they had gained a great point
in having the preaching interdicted by the
Emperor, but the infatuated men did not see that
by this written Confession, which was offered to
the Emperor, this doctrine was more preached, and
more widely propagated, than ten preachers could
have done it. It was a fine point that our preachers
were silenced, but in their stead came forth the
Elector of Saxony and other princes and lords, with
the written Confession, and preached freely in
sight of all, before the Emperor and the whole
empire. Christ surely was not silenced at the Diet,
and mad as they were, they were compelled to
hear more from the Confession, than they would
have heard from the preachers in a year. Paul's
declaration was fulfilled: 'The word of God is not
bound:' silenced in the pulpit, it was heard in the
palace; the poor preachers were not allowed to
open their lips—but great princes and lords spoke
it forth."

8. July 9, to Jonas: "There will never be agreement concerning doctrine" (between the Evangelical and Roman Churches), "for how can Christ and Belial be in concord? But the first thing, and that the greatest at this Council has been, that Christ has been proclaimed in a public and *glorious Confession*; he has been confessed in the light and to their face, so that they cannot boast that we fled, or that we feared, or concealed our faith. My only unfulfilled desire about it is that I was not present at this noble Confession. I have been like the generals who could take no part in defending Vienna from the Turks. But it is my joy and solace that meanwhile *my Vienna* was defended by others."

9. July 15, Luther addresses a letter to his "most dear brother in Christ, Spalatine, steadfast Confessor of Christ at Augsburg;" and again, July 20th, "to Spalatine, faithful servant and Confessor of Christ at Augsburg."

10. July 20, to Melanchthon: "It was a great affliction to me that I could not be present with you in the body at that most beautiful and holy Confession of Christ" (*pulcherima et sanctissima*). August 3d, he sends a letter to Melanchthon, "his most dear brother in Christ, and Confessor of the Lord at Augsburg."

11. But perhaps nowhere has Luther's enthusiastic admiration for the Augsburg Confession blazed up more brightly than in his eloquent summary of what our Confessors had done at the Diet. It is in the last letter he wrote to Melanchthon, before they again met at Coburg (September 15th): "You have confessed Christ, you

have offered peace, you have obeyed the Emperor, you have endured injuries, you have been drenched in their reviling, you have not returned evil for evil. In brief, you have worthily done God's holy work as becomes saints. Be glad then in the Lord, and exult, ye righteous. Long have ye borne witness in the world, look up and lift up your heads, for your redemption draws nigh. *I will canonize you as faithful members of Christ*, and what greater glory can ye have than to have yielded Christ faithful service, and shown yourself a member worthy of him?"

12. In his Table Talk Luther said: "Such is the efficacy and power of God's word, that the more it is persecuted, the more it flourishes and spreads. Call to mind the Diet at Augsburg, where the last trumpet before the judgment-day sounded. How the whole world then raged against our doctrine! Our doctrine and faith were brought forth to light in our Confession. Our doctrines fell into the souls of many of the noblest men, and ran like sparks in tinder. They were kindled, and kindled others. Thus our Confession and Defense came forth in the highest glory."

13. In the year 1533, Luther united in demanding of candidates as a prerequisite to entering the ministry, the declaration, "that they embraced the uncorrupted doctrine of the Gospel, and so understood it, as it is set forth in the Apostles', Nicene, and Athanasian Creeds, and as it is repeated in the Confession, which our Churches offered to the Emperor at the Diet of Augsburg, 1530, and promise that with God's help they will

remain steadfast in that conviction to the end, and will faithfully perform their duty in the Church."

It is not wonderful that Melanchthon himself considered the Confession as rather Luther's than his own, and called it "the Confession of the revered Doctor Luther."

This, then, is the result of the whole: The Holy Ghost in His ordinary illumination through the Word, is the true source and original of the Augsburg Confession; its secondary source is the whole Evangelical Church of 1530, the main organ of whose utterance was, as to the *matter* and the substance of the form, Luther; as to the finish and grace of the form, Melanchthon. Melanchthon was its composer, Luther, by pre-eminence, as the divinely called representative of the Church, its author, and hence all candid writers have most heartily indorsed Luther's own declaration, in which he not only claims the Augsburg Confession as his own, but ranks it among his most precious works: "The Catechism, the Exposition of the Ten Commandments, and the *Augsburg Confession are mine.*"

But are there not a few words of Luther in regard to the Confession, which are in conflict with this enthusiastic approval? We reply, there is not one word of the kind. The words which have been so tortured, only show that Luther wished that among the Articles on Abuses there should have been a declaration that the Pope is Antichrist, and a full handling of the doctrine of Purgatory. But the Confession, as a conjoint public document, could only discuss what a majority of those who were to unite in it thought best to present.

Melanchthon himself was overruled in regard to matters he desired to introduce. The Augsburg Confession was no private document, but in the labors of both Luther and Melanchthon in connection with it, both were the organs of the whole Church, and were compelled to sacrifice their mere private preferences to the common judgment. Every sentence, every word of the Augsburg Confession as it stands, embodies the faith of Luther, and received his unqualified, repeated, and enthusiastic assent.

If, in the Declaration of Independence, Thomas Jefferson, in preparing his statement of the political abuses which justified our separation from Great Britain, had wished to specify one or two more than the Committee thought necessary, and which were consequently not inserted, it would not weaken his claim to the authorship of that document. Nor would the fact, that he continued to think that it would have improved it to have specified the one or two additional abuses, affect the conscientious heartiness with which he indorsed that document, nor impair the value of his testimony. But even the preference of Luther, to which this is a fair parallel, was but transient, and he came to see clearly what the whole world has since seen, that in its silence, the Augsburg Confession is a model of exquisite judgment, as in its utterances it is a masterpiece of style.

9. OBJECT OF THE AUGSBURG CONFESSION

The occasion of the Augsburg Confession was the command of the Emperor,—not that he demanded such a Confession, but that under the leadings of God's providence it grew out of his summons. The last was destined to become first, and the first last. The Confessors themselves did not at first realize the full value of the opening which had been made for the proclamation of the truth, but when it dawned upon them they showed themselves worthy of their great position. They at first meant but an Apology. The faith they cherished, and the usages they practiced, they simply wished to defend from the current libels. This object they did not lose sight of, but it became secondary. Their distinctive object soon became the setting forth the great points in the whole system of heavenly truth, and the showing how, in its light, they had endeavored cautiously, and gently, yet firmly to remove the abuses which had arisen in the Church of the West. The Apology was transfigured into a Confession. It was not only not meant to be a compromise with Popery, but it clearly showed, and was designed to show, that such a compromise is impossible. Our Reformers had indeed cherished a noble hope, which bitter experience was constantly rendering feebler, that the whole Church of the West, redeemed from the thrall of the Pope, might return to her ancient Scriptural faith, and, abjuring Roman Catholicism, attain once more to Christian Catholicity, and become a Communion of saints. If such a return had been possible, the Augsburg Confession, alike in the simplicity and purity of its statement of doctrine, the conservatism of its whole tone, its firmness and its gentleness, would have helped to facilitate it; but the bridge it made, was not meant to open the way back to error, but to aid men to come over to the pure faith.

10. THE PRESENTATION OF THE CONFESSION: LATIN AND GERMAN TEXT

The Confession, in Latin and German, was presented to the Diet on Saturday, June 25th, 1530. Both texts are originals; neither text, is properly a translation of the other; both present precisely the same doctrines, but with verbal differences, which make the one an indispensable guide in the full understanding of the other; both texts have, consequently, the same authority. The German copy was the one selected, on national grounds, to be read aloud. Both copies were taken by the Emperor, who handed the German to the Elector of Mentz, and retained the Latin. It is not now known where either of the originals is, nor with certainty that either is in existence. In addition to seven unauthorized editions in the year 1530, the Confession was printed, under Melanchthon's own direction, both in Latin and German, while the Diet was still sitting. Authorized editions of this year, both in Latin and German, are in the hands of the writer, and have been examined in preparing this work. The Confession began to be multiplied at once. Innumerable editions of the originals, and translations into the chief languages of Europe appeared. Its enemies have helped its friends to circulate it, and to preserve the reissues of these originals from any change involving more than questions of purely literary interest.

11. THE AUGSBURG CONFESSION ALTERED

When Melanchthon, in 1540, issued a varied Edition of the Latin, though he declared that the changes were but verbal, and that he designed only to state more clearly the precise doctrine of the Confession in its original shape, the changes were marked by foe and friend. The Romanists at once brought the charge that Melanchthon had changed, not merely the phraseology, but the meaning of the Confession. The Calvinists and Crypto-Calvinists showed that they did not believe Melanchthon's statement that no alteration of doctrine had been intended. In the Lutheran Church different views were taken of the matter. Those who believed Melanchthon's declaration that the changes were purely verbal, the better to express the very doctrine set forth at Augsburg, either passed them over without disapproval, or were comparatively lenient in their censure. Every instance of the seeming toleration of them in the Lutheran Church was connected with the supposition that the Altered Confession in no respect whatever differed from the doctrine of the Unaltered. There never was any part of the Lutheran Church which imagined that Melanchthon had any right to alter the meaning of the Confession in a single particular. Melanchthon himself repeatedly, after the appearance of the *Variata*, acknowledged the Unaltered Augsburg Confession as a statement of his own unchanged faith, as for example, at the Diet of Ratisbon in 1541. In 1557, at the Colloquy at Worms, he not only acknowledged as his Creed, the Unaltered

Augsburg Confession, the Apology, and the
Smalcald Articles, but by name, and in writing,
condemned the Zwinglian doctrine. But a few days
before his death (1560), he said: "I confess no other
doctrine than that which Luther propounded, and
in this will abide to the end of my life." Any man
who professes to accept the Altered Confession
therefore, though he rejects the Unaltered, either is
dishonest, or assumes that Melanchthon was, and
shows himself willing to take advantage of his
moral weakness. The history of the Altered
Confession demonstrates that not only is it no gain
to the peace of the Church, but produces a yet
more grievous disturbance of it, when the effort is
made to harmonize men by an agreement in
ambiguous phraseology, the adoption of terms
which are to be accepted in one sense by one set of
men, and in another sense by another.

12. THE CURRENT EDITIONS OF THE AUGSBURG CONFESSION: LATIN AND GERMAN

The Current Edition of the Augsburg
Confession in LATIN, the one which is found in the
Book of Concord, is the reprint of Melanchthon's
own first Edition of 1530. The Current Edition of
the Confession in GERMAN, however, which is the
one found in the Book of Concord, is not a reprint
of Melanchthon's first Edition, and this fact
requires some explanation.

The original German was, as we have seen,
deposited in the imperial archives at Mentz. The
Emperor had forbidden the Confession to be
printed without his permission; nevertheless it

appeared surreptitiously several times in the year, printed in no case from a copy of the original, but from copies of the Confession made before it had reached the perfect form in which it was actually presented to the Diet. These editions of the Confession not only being unauthorized, but not presenting it in the shape in which it had actually been delivered, Melanchthon issued the Confession both in German and Latin. The German was printed from his own manuscript, from which the copy had been taken to be laid before the Diet. It reached Augsburg and was read and circulated there, while the Diet was still in session. Melanchthon issued it expressly in view of the fact that the unauthorized editions were not accurate.

The first authorized edition, the *editio princeps*, coming from the hand of its composer, and presenting not only in the nature of the case the highest guarantee for strict accuracy, but surrounded by jealous and watchful enemies, in the very Diet yet sitting, before which it was read, surrounded by men eager to mark and to exaggerate the slightest appearance of discrepancy, was received by Luther and the whole Lutheran Church. Luther knew no other Augsburg Confession in the German than this. It was received into the Bodies of Doctrine of the whole Church. It appears in the Jena edition of Luther's works, an edition which originated in the purpose of having his writings in a perfectly unchanged form, and was there given as the authentic Confession in antithesis to all the editions of it in which there were variations large or small.

In the Convention of the Evangelical (Lutheran) Princes at Naumberg in 1561, among whom were two of the original signers, this edition was declared to be authentic, and was again solemnly subscribed, and the seals of the signers appended. Nothing could seem to be more certainly fixed than that this original edition of Melanchthon presented the Confession in its most perfect form, just as it was actually delivered in the Diet.

But unhappy causes, connected largely with Melanchthon's later attempts to produce unity by skillful phrases and skillful concealments, led to a most groundless suspicion, that even in the original edition there might be variations from the very letter of the Confession as actually delivered. That there were any changes in meaning was not even in those times of morbid jealousy pretended, but a strong anxiety was felt to secure a copy of the Confession perfectly corresponding in words, in letters, and in points, with the original. The original of the Latin had been taken by Charles with him, but the German original was still supposed to be there, placed in the archives at Mentz. Joachim II, in 1566, directed Coelestinus and Zochius to make a copy from the Mentz original. Their copy was inserted in the Brandenburg Body of Doctrine in 1572. In 1576, Augustus of Saxony obtained from the Elector of Mentz, a copy of the same document, and from this the Augsburg Confession as it appears in the Book of Concord was printed. Wherever the Book of Concord was received, Melanchthon's original edition of the German was displaced, though the corresponding edition of the Latin has been retained. Thus half a century after its universal recognition, the first edition of the Augsburg Confession in German gave way to what was believed to be a true transcript of the original.

Two hundred years after the delivery of the Confession, a discovery was communicated to the theological world by Pfaff, which has reinstated Melanchthon's original edition. Pfaff discovered that the document in the archives at Mentz was not the original, but a copy merely, and the labors of Weber have demonstrated that this copy has no claim to be regarded as made from the original, but is a transcript from one of the less finished copies of the Confession, made before it had assumed, under Melanchthon's hand, the exact shape in which it was actually presented. While therefore the ordinary edition of the Augsburg Confession, the one found in the Book of Concord, and from which the current translations of the Confession have been made, does not differ in meaning at all from the original edition of Melanchthon, it is, nevertheless, not so perfect in style, and where they differ, not so clear. The highest critical authority, then, both German and Latin, is that of Melanchthon's own original editions.

The current edition of the German, and the earliest edition of Melanchthon, are verbally identical in the largest part of the articles, both of doctrine and of abuses. The only difference is, that Melanchthon's edition is occasionally somewhat fuller, especially on the abuses, is more perfectly parallel with the Latin at a few points, and occasionally more finished in style. When the question between them has a practical interest, it is simply because Melanchthon's edition expresses in terms, or with greater clearness, what is simply implied, or less explicitly stated in the other.

The translation here given is from the LATIN ORIGINAL EDITION, with the most important additions from the German in brackets. These additions are common to *both texts of the German.*

13. STRUCTURE AND DIVISIONS OF THE AUGSBURG CONFESSION

The structure of the Augsburg Confession bears traces of the mode of its growth out of the Articles which formed its groundwork. It contains, as its two fundamental parts, a positive assertion of the most necessary truths, and a negation of the most serious abuses. It comprises: I. THE PREFACE; II. TWENTY-ONE PRINCIPAL ARTICLES OF FAITH; III. AN EPILOGUE-PROLOGUE, which unites the first part with the second, and makes a graceful transition from the one to the other; IV. THE SECOND GREAT DIVISION, embracing SEVEN ARTICLES ON ABUSES; V. THE EPILOGUE, followed by the SUBSCRIPTIONS.

The ARTICLES are not arranged as a whole with reference to a system. They may be classified thus:

I. The CONFESSEDLY CATHOLIC, or Universal Christian Articles, those which Christendom, Greek and Roman, have confessed, especially in the Apostles' and Nicene Creed. These were the doctrines of the Trinity (I), the Incarnation (III), the Second Coming of Christ, the General Resurrection, the Eternity of Rewards and Punishments (XVII), the Validity of Administration by Unworthy Ministers (VIII), the Offer of Grace in Baptism, and the Right of Children to it (IX), Church Government (XIV), Civil Government (XVI), Free Will (XVIII), and the Cause of Sin (XIX).

II. The PROTESTANT Articles,—those opposed to the errors in doctrine, and the abuses in usage, of the Papal part of the Church of the West. To this the Confession, in its whole argument, based upon the Holy Scriptures as a supreme rule of faith, was opposed. But more particularly to the Pelagianism of Rome, in the doctrine of Original Sin (Art. II): its corruption of the doctrine of Justification (Art. IV): its doctrine of Merit in Works (Art. VI, XX), of the Ministerial Office, as an Order of Priests (Art. V), of Transubstantiation (Art. X), of Auricular Confession (Art. XI), of Repentance (Art. XII), of the *Opus Operatum* in Sacraments (Art. XIII), of Church Order (Art. XX), of the very nature of the Christian Church (Art. VII), and of the Worship of Saints (Art. XXI).

The entire second part was devoted to the argument against the Abuses in the Church of Rome, especially in regard to Communion in One Kind (Abus., Art. I), Celibacy of the Priesthood (Art. II), the Mass (Art. III), Confession (IV), Human Traditions (V), Monastic Vows (VI), Church Power, and especially the Jurisdiction of the Bishops (VII).

III. The EVANGELICAL Articles, or parts of Articles,—those articles which especially assert the doctrines which are connected most directly with the Gospel in its essential character as tidings of redemption to lost man,—the great doctrines of grace. These articles are specially those which teach the fall of man, the radical corruption of his nature, his exposure to eternal death, and the absolute necessity of regeneration (Art. II); the atonement of Christ, and the saving work of the Holy Spirit (Art. III); justification by faith alone (IV), the true character of repentance, or conversion (XII); and the impotence of man's own will to effect it (XVIII).

IV. The articles which set forth DISTINCTIVE BIBLICAL doctrines which the LUTHERAN Church holds in peculiar purity, over against the corruptions of Roman Catholicism, the extravagance of Radicalism, the perversions of Rationalism, or the imperfect development of theology. Such are the doctrines of the proper inseparability of the two natures of Christ, both as to time and space (Art. III), the objective force of the Word and Sacraments (Art. V), the reality of the presence of both the heavenly and earthly elements in the Lord's Supper (Art. X), the true value of Private, that is, of individual Absolution (Art. XI), the genuine character of Sacramental grace (Art. XIII), the true medium in regard to the rites of the Church (Art. XV), and the freedom of the will (XVIII), and the proper doctrine concerning the Cause of Sin (XIX). On all these points the Augsburg Confession presents views which, either in matter or measure, are opposed to extremes, which claim to be Protestant and Evangelical. Pelagianizing, Rationalistic, Fatalistic, Fanatical, unhistorical tendencies, which, more or less unconsciously, have revealed themselves, both in Roman Catholicism and in various types of nominally Evangelical Protestantism, are all met and condemned by the letter, tenor, or spirit of these articles.

Through the whole flows a spirit of earnest faith and of pure devotion. The body of the Confession shows the hand of consummate theologians, its soul reveals the inmost life of humble, earnest Christians.

14. THE LITERATURE OF THE AUGSBURG CONFESSION

The books that have been written on or about the Augsburg Confession would, in themselves, form a large library. The most important of them may be thus classified:

I. The LITERATURE of the Confession; in works of a general character; and in special works.

II. COLLECTED works, bearing on its History and Interpretation.

III. INTERPRETATION of the Confession: official writings which prepared the way for it; Manuscripts, Latin and German; Editions and Translations; Commentaries, Notes, and Sermons.

IV. Works on DOGMATICS, POLEMICS, SYMBOLIC, IRENIC, or the History of them, of value in its interpretation or defense, or as illustrating the theology based upon or deviating from it.

V. Works connected with its HISTORY.

VI. PRACTICAL and DEVOTIONAL works based upon it.

15. THE AUGSBURG CONFESSION AS A CREED:
WHAT IS INVOLVED IN A RIGHT RECEPTION OF
IT?

The very heart of all the agitation of our Church in this country lies in this question: Can we honorably bear the name of Evangelical Lutherans, honestly profess to receive the Augsburg Confession as our Creed, and honestly claim to be part of the Church of our fathers, while we reject, or leave open to rejection, parts of the doctrine whose reception gave our Church her separate being and distinctive name, and led to the formation of her Confession, and which are embodied in its articles, and guarded in their condemnatory clauses, and which our whole Church, for centuries, in every official act, maintained as principal and fundamental? This is the real question. All others are side issues. This question, once agitated, can never be laid till it is fairly settled; and to it, every conscientious man, every lover of our Church, should bend his prayerful thoughts. A testimony bearing upon the great question, a testimony of the highest importance, and entitled to be heard first of all, is the CONFESSION itself, about whose claims so much is now said.

In what light is the Augsburg Confession regarded in the Augsburg Confession itself? This is a primary question for an honest man who thinks of subscribing it; for if the Confession itself, in its origin, its history, its letter, protests against certain ideas, it would seem that its witness against them is of more value than any other. Look, then, at a few facts:

I. The Confession exhibited the one, undivided faith of the entire Lutheran Church in the Empire. It was not the work of men without authority to represent the Church; but was voice of all the Churches. Its groundwork was laid by Luther; materials were brought together by the great theologians of the whole Lutheran Church—by Brentius, Jonas, Spalatine, and others, who carefully examined, and Melanchthon was employed in giving the most perfect form, the most absolutely finished statement of the faith; the Confession was subjected to the careful examination of Luther, by whom it was heartily approved. Melanchthon's own account is: "I brought together the heads of the Confession, embracing almost the *sum of the doctrine of our churches.* I took nothing on myself. In the presence of the Princes and the officials, every topic was discussed by our preachers *sentence by sentence. A copy of the entire Confession* was then sent to Luther, who wrote to the Princes, that he had read, and that he approved the Confession." Every position of the Confession had been pondered again and again, had been tried in the crucible of the Word, had been experienced in its practical power in the life, and had been maintained against sharp attacks, by our great Confessors, as well as by thousands of humble and earnest private Christians. For the immediate work of its preparation, there were at least four months. It was on the 11th of May the Confession was sent by the Elector to Luther, and it was not read in Diet till the 25th of June; so that *six weeks elapsed* between the time of its completion and of its presentation. Every touch after that time, was simply that of the file, the result of Melanchthon's striving after absolute finish of style. Never was a Confession more thoroughly prepared, more carefully and prayerfully weighed, more heartily accepted.

II. As various kingdoms, states, and cities embraced the faith of God's word, as our Church had unfolded it, they accepted this Confession as their own, and were known as Evangelical Lutherans, because they so accepted it. The Church was known as the Church of the Augsburg Confession, and that great document became a part of the defining terms of the Church. The Lutheran Church was that which unreservedly held the Unaltered Augsburg Confession in its historical sense.

III. The arguments on which men rely now to shake the faith of the Church, had all been used before the Confession was prepared. In fact, the Rationalistic argument had been brought out with far more vigor and plausibility, than usually attend it now, and those who renew the unsuccessful attempts of the original opponents of our faith, might with advantage to their cause study those old errorists. Nothing has been added to the argument of that day in the great substantial points on either side. After the learning and insinuating statement of Œolampadius, whose work, Erasmus said, "might, if possible, deceive the very elect," and which Melanchthon considered worthy of a reply—after the unflinching audacity of Carlstadt, and the plausible argument of

Zwingli, which was so shallow, and therefore seemed so clear, it is not probable that the feeble echo of their arguments which is now alone heard in the maintenance of their views, would shake our fathers were they living. The Scripture argument stands now where it stood then, and the Word, which was too strong for Luther's human doubts then, would prove too strong for them now. It is not the argument which has changed: it is as overwhelming now as then; but the singleness of faith, the simple-hearted trust—these have too often yielded to the Rationalizing spirit of a vain and self-trusting generation. If our fathers, with their old spirit, were living now, we would have to stand with them, on their Confession, or be obliged to stand alone. Luther would sing now, as he sung then:

> "The Word they shall permit remain,
> And not a thank have for it."

IV. The very name of AUGSBURG, which tells us WHERE our Confession was uttered, reminds us of the nature of the obligations of those who profess to receive it. Two other Confessions were brought to that city: the Confession of Zwingli, and the Tetrapolitan Confession: the former openly opposed to the faith of our Church, especially in regard to the Sacraments; the latter ambiguous and evasive on some of the vital points of the same doctrine. These two Confessions are now remembered only because of the historical glory shed by ours over everything which came into any relation to it. But can it be, that the doctrine which arrayed itself against the Augsburg Confession at

Augsburg can be the doctrine of that Confession, or capable of harmonizing with it anywhere else; that what was not Lutheranism there is Lutheranism here; that what was Lutheranism then is not Lutheranism now; that Zwingli or Hedio of Strasburg could, without a change of views, honestly subscribe the Confession against which they had arrayed themselves, that very Confession, the main drift of some of whose most important Articles was to teach the truth these men denied, and to condemn the errors these men fostered, or that men, who hold now what they held then, can now honestly do what they would not and could not do then? What could not be done then, cannot be done now. A principle is as little affected by the lapse of three hundred years as of one year. It cannot be, that, consistently with the principles of our fathers, consistently with Church unity with them, consistently with the Church name which their principles and their faith defined, men holding Roman, or Rationalistic, or Zwinglian error, should pretend to receive the Confession as their own. Such a course effaces all the lines of historical identity, and of moral consistency, and opens the way to error of every kind.

V. The language of the Confession, when it speaks of itself, is well worthy of attention.

1. It calls itself a *Confession*, not a rule. The Bible is the only rule of faith, and this document *confesses* the faith of which the Bible is the rule.

2. It calls itself a Confession of *faith*; of *faith*, not of men's opinions or views, but of that divine conviction of saving truth, which the Holy Ghost

works through the Word. It speaks of that with
which it has to do as "the holy faith and Christian
religion," "the one only and true religion," "our
holy religion and Christian faith." The title of the
doctrinal portion of the Confession is, "*Principal
Articles of Faith.*"

3. The Confessors speak of this Confession of
faith as "the Confession of their *preachers*, and
their own Confession," "the doctrine which *their
preachers* have presented and taught in the
Churches, in their lands, principalities, and cities."
The Preface closes with the words: "This is the
Confession of *ourselves* and of *ours*, as now
distinctly follows, Article by Article." They
separate *their* faith alike from the errors of Rome
and of the fanatical and rationalizing tendencies of
the day.

4. The Confession declares that: "The
CHURCHES among us teach" the doctrines set forth
in the Articles. It is not simply great princes, nor
great theologians; it is the CHURCHES which teach
these doctrines. The private opinions of the
greatest of men are here nothing. It is the faith of
the Churches which is set forth, and those who
acted for them spoke as their representatives,
knowing the common faith, and not mingling with
it any mere private sentiments or peculiar views of
their own, however important they might regard
them.

It is a great mistake to suppose that our
Evangelical Protestant Church is bound by
consistency to hold a view simply because Luther
held it. Her faith is not to be brought to the
touchstone of Luther's private opinion, but his

private opinion is to be tested by her confessed faith, when the question is, What is genuinely Lutheran? The name Lutheran, as our Church tolerates it, means no more than that she heartily accepts that New Testament faith in its integrity, in whose restoration Luther was so glorious a leader. When, at the conferences at Augsburg, Eck produced certain passages from Luther's writings, Brentius and Schnepf replied: "We are not here to defend Luther's writings, but to maintain our Confession." In showing that the Augsburg Confession is the Symbol of our time, the Formula of Concord rests its authority on its being "the unanimous consent and declaration of our faith." The private opinions of individuals, however influential, can in no sense establish or remove one word of the Creed of the Church Any man, who, on any pretense, gives ecclesiastical authority to private opinions, is robbing the Church of her freedom. She is to be held responsible for no doctrines which she has not officially declared to be her own.

5. The Confessors say, at the end of the doctrinal Articles: "This is almost *the main portion (summa: chief points, principal matters) of the doctrine* which is preached and taught in our Churches, in order to the true Christian instruction and comfort of the conscience, as also for the edification of believers." It calls the things it sets forth "the one, simple truth," and styles them "the chief," or fundamental, "Articles" (Hauptartikeln).

The Confessors style and characterize the Confession as "our Confession," as "the *chief points* of the doctrine taught in our Churches," as "the main (or fundamental) Articles," as "the Articles of faith." They say: "*Those things only have been recited* which seemed *necessary* to be said, that it might be understood, that, in *doctrine* and ceremonies, *nothing* is received by us *contrary to Scripture*;" and they declare, at the close of their work, that it was meant as "a sum of doctrine," or statement of its chief points, "for the making known of our Confession, and of the doctrine of those who teach among us."

6. The Confessors say of this statement of the main points of doctrine: "In it may be seen, *that there is* NOTHING *which departs from the Scriptures*;" "it is clearly founded in the holy Scriptures," "in conformity with the pure, Divine word and Christian truth." They declare, that, in these "main" or fundamental "Articles, no falsity or deficiency is to be found, and that this their Confession is godly and Christian (göttlich und Christlich)." They open the Articles on Abuses by reiterating, that their Confession is evidence, that, "in the *Articles of faith*, NOTHING is taught in our Churches contrary to the Holy Scripture," and the Confessors close with the declaration, that, if there be points on which the Confession has not touched, they are prepared to furnish ample information, "in accordance with the Scriptures," "on the ground of holy Divine writ."

7. The Confessors say that in the Confession: "There is NOTHING which departs from the *Church Catholic, the Universal Christian Church.*"

8. The Confessors moreover declare, that they set forth their Confession that they may "not put their soul and conscience in the very highest and

greatest peril before God by abuse of the Divine name or word."

9. They declare, moreover, that it is their grand design in the Confession, to avoid the "transmission as *a heritage* to their *children and descendants* of *another doctrine*, a doctrine not in conformity with the pure Divine word and Christian truth."

Our fathers knew well that human opinions fluctuate, that men desert the truth, that convictions cannot be made hereditary; but they knew this also, that when men assume a name, they assume the obligations of the name, that they may not honestly subscribe Confessions unless they believe their contents; and they knew that after this, their great Confession, men could not long keep up the pretense of being of them who were anti-Trinitarian, Pelagian, Roman, Rationalistic, or Fanatical. They could transmit the heritage of their faith to their children, trusting in God that these children would not, for the brassy glitter of Rationalism, or the scarlet rags of Rome, part with this birthright, more precious than gold.

Our lathers believed, with St. Paul, that the true faith is "one faith," and, therefore, never changes. It is the same from age to age. The witness of a true faith is a witness to the end of time. When, therefore, Brück, the Chancellor of Saxony, presented the Confession, he said: "By the help of God and of our Lord Jesus Christ, this Confession shall remain invincible, against the gates of hell, TO ETERNITY!"

16. THE CHARACTER AND VALUE OF THE
AUGSBURG CONFESSION

The Augsburg Confession was exquisitely adapted to all its objects, as a Confession of faith, and a Defense of it. In it the very heart of the Gospel beat again. It gave organic being to what had hitherto been but a tendency, and knit together great nationalities in the holiest bond by which men can be held in association. It enabled the Evangelical Princes, as a body, to throw their moral weight for truth into the Empire. These were the starting-points of its great work and glory among men. To it, under God, more than to any other cause, the whole Protestant world owes civil and religious freedom. Under it, as a banner, the pride of Rome was broken, and her armies destroyed. It is the symbol of pure Protestantism, as the three General Creeds are symbols of that developing Catholicity to which genuine Protestantism is related, as the maturing fruit is related to the blossom. To it the eyes of all deep thinkers have been turned, as to a star of hope amid the internal strifes of nominal Protestantism. Gieseler, the great Reformed Church historian, says: "If the question be, Which, among all Protestant Confessions, is best adapted for forming the foundation of a union among Protestant Churches, we declare ourselves unreservedly for the Augsburg Confession." But no genuine union can ever be formed upon the basis of the Augsburg Confession, except by a hearty consent in its whole faith, an honest reception of all its statements of doctrine in the sense which the statements bear in the Confession itself. If there be those who would forgive Rome her unrepented sins, they must do it in the face of the Augsburg Confession. If there be those who would consent to a truce at least with Rationalism or Fanaticism, they must begin their work by making men forget the great Confession, which refused its covert to them from the beginning. With the Augsburg Confession begins the clearly recognized life of the Evangelical Protestant Church, the purified Church of the West, on which her enemies fixed the name Lutheran. With this Confession her most self-sacrificing struggles and greatest achievements are connected. It is hallowed by the prayers of Luther, among the most ardent that ever burst from the human heart; it is made sacred by the tears of Melanchthon, among the tenderest which ever fell from the eyes of man. It is embalmed in the living, dying, and undying devotion of the long line of the heroes of our faith, who, through the world which was not worthy of them, passed to their eternal rest. The greatest masters in the realm of intellect have defended it with their labors; the greatest princes have protected it from the sword, by the sword; and the blood of its martyrs, speaking better things than vengeance, pleads forever, with the blood of Him whose all-availing love, whose sole and all-atoning sacrifice, is the beginning, middle, and end of its witness.

But not alone on the grand field of historical events has its power been shown. It led to God's Word millions, who have lived and died unknown to the great world. In the humblest homes and humblest hearts it has opened, through ages, the spring of heavenly influence. It proclaimed the all-sufficiency of Christ's merits, the justifying power of faith in Him; and this shed heavenly light, peace and joy on the darkest problems of the burdened heart. "It remains forever," says Gieseler, "a light to guide in the right path those who are struggling in error." It opened the way to the true unity of the Church of Christ; and if it has seemed to divide, for a little time, it has divided only to consolidate at length, the whole Church, under Christ's sole rule, and in the one pure faith.

Its history, in its full connections, is the history of the centuries midway in the fourth of which we stand, and the future of the Church, which is the future of the race, can unfold itself from the present, only in the power of the life which germinates from the great principles which the Augsburg Confession planted in the world.

17. OBJECT AND CHARACTER OF THE PRESENT WORK

The distinctive peculiarities of this Edition of the Augsburg Confession are these:

First. After the THREE GENERAL CREEDS, which are presupposed as an historical foundation, it gives a LITERAL TRANSLATION of the Confession from the LATIN, with the most important additions from the GERMAN [in brackets].

Second. The Articles are reduced to a UNIFORM NUMERATION from One to Twenty-eight, with a SECOND NUMBER marking the Articles on Abuses as such.

Third. The Articles are divided into PARAGRAPHS, each one of which contains a distinct thought. These are numbered in correspondence with the best editions of the original, so as to facilitate reference.

Fourth. It furnishes, in an INTRODUCTION, a new collection of materials for an understanding of the origin and character of the Confession, and also gives REFERENCES to the chief original SOURCES of its history.

Fifth. In a series of NOTES, it endeavors, chiefly by official evidence, to remove the most important misapprehensions of the meaning of the Confession. It gives, in this connection, the titles of other works in English, in which the same topics are treated.

Sixth. It gives a more THOROUGH INDEX of the Confession, than, so far as the writer knows, has ever been prepared before, in fact, to a large extent, a CONCORDANCE of its most important words. This INDEX is meant as an aid in making the Confession its own interpreter.

Seventh. This Edition, while it excludes what could be interesting to the scholar merely, has endeavored to compress within a moderate compass what will be of most general utility to our ministers and people. It is designed as an humble aid, by God's help, in the work of deepening an intelligent devotion to the great doctrines of His Word, the doctrines which have been the life of His Church, the revival of which created the Reformation, and the conservation of which, as the only hope of the world, is the holiest duty of those who love the faith once delivered to the Saints.

.

PART I

THE ECUMENICAL CREEDS

THE THREE ECUMENICAL CREEDS

I. THE APOSTLES' CREED

1. I believe in God, the Father Almighty, Maker of heaven and earth:

2. And in Jesus Christ, his only Son, our Lord,

3. Who was conceived by the Holy Ghost,

4. Born of the Virgin Mary, suffered under Pontius Pilate, Was crucified, dead, and buried:

5. He descended into Hell, the third day he rose again from the dead, He ascended into heaven, And sitteth on the right hand of God the Father Almighty;

6. From thence he shall come to judge the quick and the dead.

7. I believe in the Holy Ghost; the holy Catholic [Christian] Church, the Communion of Saints; The forgiveness of sins;

8. The Resurrection of the body, And the life everlasting. Amen.

II. THE NICENE CREED

1. I believe in one God, the Father Almighty, Maker of heaven and earth, And of all things visible and invisible.

2. And in one Lord Jesus Christ, the only-begotten Son of God,

3. Begotten of his Father, before all Worlds, God of God, Light of Light, Very God of very God,

Begotten, not made, Being of one Substance with the Father; By whom all things were made,

4. Who for us men, and for our salvation came down from heaven, And was incarnate by the Holy Ghost of the Virgin Mary, and was made man,

5. And was crucified also for us under Pontius Pilate. He suffered and was buried, And the third day he rose again according to the Scriptures, And ascended into heaven, And sitteth on the right hand of the Father.

6. And he shall come again with glory to judge both the quick and the dead: Whose kingdom shall have no end.

7. And I believe in the Holy Ghost, The Lord and Giver of life, Who proceedeth from the Father and the Son, Who with the Father and the Son together is worshipped and glorified, Who spake by the Prophets.

8. And I believe in one holy, Catholic [Christian] and Apostolic Church.

9. I acknowledge one Baptism for the remission of sins,

10. And I look for the Resurrection of the dead, and the life of the world to come. Amen.

III. THE CREED OF ATHANASIUS

WRITTEN AGAINST THE ARIANS

1. Whosoever will be saved, before all things it is necessary that he hold the Catholic [true Christian] faith,

2. Which Faith except every one do keep whole and undefiled, without doubt he shall perish everlastingly.

3. And the Catholic [true Christian] faith is this: that we worship one God in Trinity, and Trinity in Unity;

4. Neither confounding the Persons; nor dividing the Substance.

5. For there is one Person of the Father, another of the Son, and another of the Holy Ghost.

6. But the Godhead of the Father, of the Son, and of the Holy Ghost, is all one: the Glory Equal, the Majesty Coeternal.

7. Such as the Father is, such is the Son: and such is the Holy Ghost.

8. The Father uncreate, the Son uncreate: and the Holy Ghost uncreate.

9. The Father incomprehensible, the Son incomprehensible: and the Holy Ghost incomprehensible.

10. The Father eternal, the Son eternal: and the Holy Ghost eternal.

11. And yet they are not three Eternals: but one Eternal.

12. As also there are not three incomprehensibles, nor three uncreated: but one eternal, and one incomprehensible.

13. So likewise the Father is Almighty, the Son Almighty: and the Holy Ghost Almighty.

14. And yet they are not three Almighties: but one Almighty.

15. So the Father is God, the Son is God: and the Holy Ghost is God.

16. And yet they are not three Gods: but one God.

17. So likewise the Father is Lord, the Son Lord: and the Holy Ghost Lord.

18. And yet not three Lords: but one Lord.

19. For like as we are compelled by the Christian verity: to acknowledge every Person by himself to be God and Lord;

So are we forbidden by the Catholic [Christian] Religion: to say, There be three Gods, or three Lords.

20. The Father is made of none: neither created nor begotten.

21. The Son is of the Father alone: not made, nor created, but begotten.

22. The Holy Ghost is of the Father, and of the Son; neither made, nor created, nor begotten, but proceeding.

23. So there is one Father, not three Fathers; one Son, not three Sons: one Holy Ghost, not three Holy Ghosts.

24. And in this Trinity none is before, or after other: none is greater, or less than another;

25. But the whole three Persons are coeternal together, and coequal: So that in all things, as is aforesaid: the Unity in Trinity, and the Trinity in Unity is to be worshipped.

26. He therefore that will be saved must thus think of the Trinity.

27. Furthermore, it is necessary to Everlasting Salvation: that we also believe rightly the Incarnation of our Lord Jesus Christ.

28. For the right Faith is, that we believe and confess: that our Lord Jesus Christ, the Son of God, is God and Man;

29. God, of the Substance of the Father begotten before the worlds: and Man of the Substance of his mother, born in the world;

30. Perfect God, and perfect Man: of a reasonable soul and human flesh subsisting.

31. Equal to the Father, as touching his Godhead: and inferior to the Father, as touching his Manhood.

32. Who although he be God and Man: yet he is not two, but one Christ;

33. One; not by conversion of the Godhead into flesh: but by taking the Manhood into God;

34. One altogether; not by confusion of Substance: but by Unity of Person.

35. For as the reasonable soul and flesh is one man: so God and Man is one Christ;

36. Who suffered for our salvation: descended into hell, rose again the third day from the dead.

37. He ascended into heaven; he sitteth on the right hand of the Father, God Almighty: from whence he shall come to judge the quick and the dead.

38. At whose coming all men shall rise again with their bodies: and shall give account for their own works.

39. And they that have done good shall go into life everlasting: and they that have done evil into everlasting fire.

40. This is the Catholic [true Christian] faith: which except a man believe faithfully, he cannot be saved.

PART II

THE AUGSBURG CONFESSION

PREFACE TO THE EMPEROR CHARLES V

I
CHIEF ARTICLES OF FAITH

II
ARTICLES IN WHICH ARE ENUMERATED THE ABUSES CORRECTED

I.   OF BOTH KINDS
II. OF THE MARRIAGE OF PRIESTS
III. OF THE MASS
IV. OF CONFESSION
V.   OF THE DISTINCTION OF MEATS, AND OF TRADITIONS
VI. OF MONASTIC VOWS
VII. OF ECCLESIASTICAL POWER. EPILOGUE

CONFESSION OF FAITH

PRESENTED TO THE INVINCIBLE EMPEROR CHARLES V,
CÆSAR AUGUSTUS, AT THE DIET OF AUGSBURG, ANNO
DOMINI MDXXX.

"I will speak of thy testimonies also before kings, and
will not be ashamed."
PSALM 119:46.

PREFACE TO THE EMPEROR CHARLES V

[1] Most Invincible Emperor, Cæsar Augustus, Most Clement Master: Inasmuch as Tour Imperial Majesty has summoned a Convention of the Empire at Augsburg, to deliberate in regard to aid against the Turk, the most atrocious, the hereditary, and ancient enemy of the Christian name and religion, in what way, to wit, resistance might be made to his rage and assaults, by protracted and perpetual preparation for war: Because, moreover, [2] of dissensions in the matter of our holy religion and Christian faith, and in order that in this matter of religion the opinions and judgments of diverse parties may be heard in each other's presence, may be understood and weighed among one another, in mutual charity, meekness, and gentleness, [3] that those things which in the writings on either side have been

handled or understood amiss, being laid aside and corrected, these things may be harmonized and brought back to the one simple truth and Christian Concord; [4] so that hereafter the one unfeigned and true religion may be embraced and preserved by us, so that as we are subjects and soldiers of the One Christ, so also, in unity and concord, we may live in the one Christian Church: and inasmuch as We, the Electors and Princes, [5] whose names are subscribed, together with others who are conjoined with us, in common with other Electors and Princes, and States, have been called to the aforenamed Diet, we have, in order to render most humble obedience to the Imperial Mandate, come early to Augsburg, and with no desire to boast would state that we were among the very first to be present.

[6] When therefore Your Imperial Majesty, among other things, has also at Augsburg, at the very beginning of these sessions, caused the proposition to be made to the Princes and States of the Empire, that each of the States of the Empire, in virtue of the Imperial Edict, should propose and offer in the German and in the Latin language its opinion and decision; [7] after discussion on Wednesday we replied to Your Imperial Majesty, that on the following Friday we would offer on our part the Articles of our Confession:

[8] Wherefore, in order that we may do homage to the will of Your Imperial Majesty, we now offer in the matter of religion the Confession of our preachers and of ourselves, the doctrine of which derived from the Holy Scriptures and pure Word of God they have to this time set forth in our

lands, dukedoms, domains, and cities, and have taught in the churches. [9] If the other Electors, Princes, and States of the Empire, should in the writings, to wit, in Latin and German, according to the aforementioned Imperial proposition, produce their opinions in this matter of religion: we here in the presence of Your Imperial Majesty our most Clement Lord, [10] offer ourselves, prepared, in conjunction with the Princes and our friends already designated, to compare views in a kindly manner in regard to mode and ways which may be available, so that as far as may honorably be done, we may agree, and the matter between us of both parts being peacefully discussed, with no hateful contention, by God's help the dissension may be removed, and may be brought back to one true accordant religion (as we are all subjects and soldiers under one Christ, [11] so also we ought to confess one Christ, in accordance with the tenor of the decree of Your Imperial Majesty), and all things should be brought back to the truth of God, which with most fervent prayers we beseech God to grant.

[12] But if, as regards the rest of Electors, Princes, and States, those of the other party, this treatment of the matter of religion, in the manner in which Your Imperial Majesty has wisely thought fit it should be conducted and treated, to wit, with such a mutual presentation of writings and calm conference between us, should not go on, nor be attended by any result; [13] yet shall we leave a clear testimony that in no manner do we evade anything which can tend to promote Christian concord (anything which God and a good

conscience allow); [14] and this Your Imperial Majesty and the other Electors and States of the Empire, and all who are moved by a sincere love of religion and concern for it, all who are willing to give an equitable hearing in this matter, will kindly gather and understand from the Confession of ourselves and of ours.

[15] Since, moreover, Your Imperial Majesty has not once only, but repeatedly signified to the Electors, Princes, and other States of the Empire; and at the Diet of Spires, which was held in the year of our Lord 1526, caused to be recited and publicly proclaimed, in accordance with the form of Your Imperial instruction and commission given and prescribed: That Your Imperial Majesty in this matter of religion for certain reasons, [16] stated in the name of Your Majesty, was not willing to determine, nor was able to conclude touching anything, but that Your Imperial Majesty would diligently endeavor to have the Roman Pontiff, in accordance with his office, to assemble a General Council: [17] as also the same matter was more amply set forth a year ago in the last public Convention, which was held at Spires, [18] where through His Highness Ferdinand, King of Bohemia and Hungary, our friend and clement Lord, afterward through the Orator and the Imperial Commissioners, Your Imperial Majesty, among other propositions, caused these to be made, that Your Imperial Majesty had known and pondered, [19] the resolution to convene a Council, formed by the Representatives of Your Imperial Majesty in the Empire, and by the Imperial President and Counsellors, and by the Legates of other States

convened at Ratisbon, and this Your Imperial
Majesty also judged that it would be useful to
assemble a Council, and because the matters which
were to be adjusted at this time between Your
Imperial Majesty and the Roman Pontiff were
approaching   agreement   and   Christian
reconciliation, Your Imperial Majesty did not doubt
that, but that the Pope could be induced to
summon a General Council: [20] Wherefore Your
Imperial Majesty signified that Your Imperial
Majesty would endeavor to bring it to pass that the
Chief Pontiff, together with Your Imperial Majesty,
would consent at the earliest opportunity to issue
letters for the convening of such a General
Council.

[21] As the event, therefore, has been that in
this matter of religion the differences between us
and the other party have not been settled in
friendship and love, we here present ourselves
before Your Imperial Majesty, in all obedience, and
in more than mere obedience, ready to compare
views, and to defend our cause in such a general,
free, and Christian Council, concerning the
convening of which, there has been concordant
action and a determination by agreeing votes on
the part of the Electors, Princes, and the other
States of the Empire, in all the Imperial Diets
which have been held in the reign of Your Imperial
Majesty. To this Convention of a General Council,
[22] as also to Your Imperial Majesty, we have in
the due method and legal form, before made our
protestation and appeal in this greatest and gravest
of matters. To which appeal both to Your Imperial
Majesty and a Council we still adhere; [23] nor do

we intend, nor would it be possible for us to forsake it by this or any other document, unless the matter between us and the other party should, in accordance with the tenor of the latest Imperial citation, be compared, settled, and brought to Christian concord, in friendship and love; [24] concerning which appeal we here also make our solemn and public protest.

I

CHIEF ARTICLES OF FAITH

ARTICLE I

Of God

[1] THE churches with common consent among us, do teach that the decree of the Nicene Synod [Council] concerning the unity of the divine essence and of the three persons is true, and without doubt to be believed: to wit, [2] that there is one divine essence which is called and is God, eternal, without body, indivisible [without part], of infinite power, wisdom, goodness, the Creator and Preserver of all things, visible and invisible; [3] and that yet there be three persons of the same essence and power, who also are coeternal, the Father, the Son, and the Holy Ghost.

[4] And they use the name of person in that signification in which the ecclesiastical writers [the fathers] have used it in this cause, to signify, not a part or quality in another, but that which properly subsists.

[5] They condemn all heresies which have sprung up against this Article, as the Manicheans, who set down two principles, good and evil; in the

same manner the Valentinians, Ariaus, Eunomians, Mahometans, and all such like.

[6] They condemn also the Samosatenes, old and new; who, when they earnestly contend that there is but one person, do craftily and wickedly trifle after the manner of Rhetoricians, about the Word and Holy Ghost, that they are not distinct persons, but that the Word signifies a vocal word, and the Spirit a motion created in things.

ARTICLE II

Of Original Sin

[1] Also they teach that after Adam's fall, all men begotten after the common course of nature, are born with sin; that is, without the fear of God, [2] without trust in him, and with fleshly appetite; [3] and that this disease, or original fault is truly sin, condemning and bringing eternal death now also upon all that are not born again by baptism and the Holy Spirit.

[4] They condemn the Pelagians, and others, who deny this original fault to be sin indeed; and who, so as to lessen the glory of the merits and benefits of Christ, argue that a man may, by the strength of his own reason, be justified before God.

ARTICLE III

Of the Son of God, and of the Holy Spirit

[1] Also they teach that the Word, that is, the Son of God took unto him man's nature, in the womb of the blessed Virgin Mary, so that there are

two natures, [2] the Divine and the human, inseparably joined together in unity of person; one Christ, true God and true man: who was born of the Virgin Mary, truly suffered, was crucified, dead, and buried, [3] that he might reconcile the Father unto us, and might be a sacrifice, not only for original guilt, but also for all actual sins of men.

[4] The same also descended into hell, and truly rose again the third day. Afterward he ascended into the heavens, that he might sit at the right hand of the Father; and reign forever, and have dominion over all creatures; might sanctify those that believe in him, by sending the Holy Spirit into their hearts, [5] who shall rule [purify, strengthen], comfort, and quicken them, and shall defend them against the devil, and the power of sin.

[6] The same Christ shall openly come again, to judge the quick and the dead, according as the Apostles' Creed declares these and other things.

ARTICLE IV

Of Justification

[1] Also they teach, that men cannot be justified [obtain forgiveness of sins and righteousness] before God by their own powers, merits, or works: [2] but are justified freely [of grace] for Christ's sake through faith, when they believe that they are received into favor, and their sins forgiven for Christ's sake, who by his death has satisfied for our sins. [3] This faith God imputes for righteousness before Him, Rom. 3 and 4.

ARTICLE V

Of the Ministry of the Church

[1] For the obtaining of this faith, the ministry of teaching the Gospel, and administering the Sacraments was instituted.

[2] For by the Word and Sacraments, as by instruments, the Holy Spirit is given; who works faith, where and when it pleases God, in those that hear the Gospel, to wit, that God, not for our merit's sake, [3] but for Christ's sake, doth justify those who believe that they for Christ's sake are received into favor.

They condemn the Anabaptists and others, [4] who imagine that the Holy Spirit is given to men without the outward word, through their own preparations and works.

ARTICLE VI

Of New Obedience

[1] Also they teach that this faith should bring forth good fruits, and that men ought to do the good works commanded of God, because it is God's will, and not on any confidence of meriting justification before God by their works.

[2] For remission of sins and justification is apprehended by faith, as also the voice of Christ witnesses: "When ye have done all these things, say, we are unprofitable servants."

The same, also, [3] do the ancient writers of the Church teach; for Ambrose said: "This is ordained of God, that he that believeth in Christ shall be saved, without works, by faith alone, freely receiving forgiveness of sins."

ARTICLE VII

Of the Church

[1] Also they teach, that one holy Church is to continue forever. But the Church is the congregation of saints [the assembly of all believers], in which the Gospel is rightly taught [purely preached], and the Sacraments rightly administered [according to the Gospel].

And unto the true unity of the Church, [2] it is sufficient to agree concerning the doctrine of the Gospel and the administration of the Sacraments. [3] Nor is it necessary that human traditions, rites, or ceremonies instituted by men, should be alike everywhere; [4] as St. 4 Paul says: "There is one faith, one baptism, one God and Father of all."

ARTICLE VIII

What the Church is?

[1] Though the Church be properly the congregation of saints and true believers, yet seeing that in this life many hypocrites and evil persons are mingled with it, it is lawful to use the Sacraments administered by evil men; according to the voice of Christ: "The Scribes and the Pharisees sit in Moses' seat," and the words following. [2] And the Sacraments and the Word are effectual, by reason of the institution and commandment of Christ, though they be delivered by evil men.

[3] They condemn the Donatists and such like, who denied that it was lawful to use the ministry of evil men in the Church, and held that the ministry of evil men is useless and without effect.

ARTICLE IX

Of Baptism

[1] Of Baptism they teach, that it is necessary to salvation, and that by Baptism the grace of God is offered, [2] and that children are to be baptized, who by Baptism, being offered to God are received into God's favor.

[3] They condemn the Anabaptists who allow not the Baptism of children, and affirm that children are saved without Baptism.

ARTICLE X

Of the Lord's Supper

[1] Of the Supper of the Lord they teach that the [true] body and blood of Christ are truly present [under the form of bread and wine], [2] and are [there] communicated to those that eat in the Lord's Supper [and received][3].

[4] And they disapprove of those that teach otherwise [wherefore also the opposite doctrine is rejected].

ARTICLE XI

Of Confession

[1] Concerning confession, they teach that private absolution be retained in the churches, though enumeration of all offences be not necessary in confession. For it is impossible; according to the Psalm: [2] "Who can understand his errors?"

ARTICLE XII

Of Repentance

[1] Touching repentance, they teach that such as have fallen after baptism may find remission of sins, at what time they are converted [when they come to repentance], [2] and that the Church should give absolution unto such as return to repentance.

[3] Now repentance consists properly of these two parts. One is contrition, [4] or terrors stricken into the conscience through the acknowledgment of sin: [5] the other is faith, which is conceived by the Gospel, or absolution, and doth believe that for Christ's sake sins be forgiven, and comforts the conscience, and frees it from terrors. Then should follow good works, [6] which are fruits of repentance.

[7] They condemn the Anabaptists, who deny that men once justified can lose the Spirit of God, [8] and do contend that some men may attain to such a perfection in this life, that they cannot sin. [Here are rejected those who teach, that those who have once been holy cannot fall again.] [9]The Novatians are also condemned, who would not absolve such as had fallen after baptism, though they returned to repentance. [10] They also that do

not teach that remission of sins is obtained by faith, and who command us to merit grace by satisfactions are rejected.

ARTICLE XIII

Of the Use of Sacraments

[1] Concerning the use of the Sacraments, they teach that they were ordained, not only to be marks of profession amongst men, but rather that they should be signs and testimonies of the will of God towards us, set forth unto us, to stir up and confirm faith in such as use them. [2] Therefore men must use Sacraments so, as to join faith with them, which believes the promises that are offered and declared unto us by the Sacraments.

[3] Wherefore they condemn those that teach that the Sacraments do justify by the work done, and do not teach that faith which believes the remission of sins is requisite in the use of Sacraments.

ARTICLE XIV

Of Ecclesiastical Orders

[1] Concerning Ecclesiastical Orders [Church Government], they teach, that no man should publicly in the Church teach, or administer the Sacraments, except he be rightly called [without a regular call].

ARTICLE XV

Of Ecclesiastical Rites

[1] Concerning Ecclesiastical rites, they teach, that those rites are to be observed, which may be observed without sin, and are profitable for tranquility and good order in the Church; such as are, set holidays, feasts, and such like. Yet concerning such things, [2] men are to be admonished, that consciences are not to be burdened as if such service were necessary to salvation.

[3] They are also to be admonished that human traditions, instituted to propitiate God, to merit grace and make satisfaction for sins, are opposed to the Gospel and the doctrine of faith. [4] Wherefore vows and traditions concerning foods and days, and such like, instituted to merit grace and make satisfaction for sins, are useless and contrary to the Gospel.

ARTICLE XVI

Of Civil Affairs

[1] Concerning civil affairs, they teach that such civil ordinances as are lawful, are good works of God; [2] that Christians may lawfully bear civil office, sit in judgments, determine matters by the imperial laws, and other laws in present force, appoint just punishments, engage in just war, act as soldiers, make legal bargains and contracts, hold property, take an oath when the magistrates require it, marry a wife, or be given in marriage. They condemn the Anabaptists, [3] who forbid Christians these civil offices. [4] They condemn

also those that place the perfection of the Gospel, not in the fear of God, and in faith, but in forsaking civil offices, inasmuch as the Gospel teaches an everlasting righteousness of the heart. [5] In the meantime, it doth not disallow order and government of commonwealths or families, but requires especially the preservation and maintenance thereof, as of God's own ordinances, and that in such ordinances we should exercise love. Christians, therefore, [6] must necessarily obey their magistrates and laws, save only then, when they command any sin; for then they must rather obey God than men. Acts 5:29.

ARTICLE **XVII**

Of Christ's Return to Judgment

[1] Also they teach that, in the consummation of the world [at the last day], Christ shall appear to judge, and shall raise up all the dead, and shall give unto the godly and elect, eternal life, and everlasting joys; but ungodly men and the devils shall he condemn unto endless torments.

[2] They condemn the Anabaptists, who think that to condemned men and the devils shall be an end of torments. They condemn others also, [3] who now scatter Jewish opinions, that, before the resurrection of the dead, the godly shall occupy the kingdom of the world, the wicked being everywhere suppressed [the saints alone, the pious, shall have a worldly kingdom, and shall exterminate all the godless].

ARTICLE **XVIII**

Of Free Will

[1] Concerning free will, they teach, that man's will hath some liberty to work a civil righteousness, and to choose such things as reason can reach unto: [2] but that it hath no power to work the righteousness of God, or a spiritual righteousness, without the Spirit of God; because that the natural man receives not the things of the Spirit of God: 1 Cor. 2:14. [3] But this is wrought in the heart when men do receive the Spirit of God through the word.

[4] These things are in as many words affirmed by St. Augustine, *Hypognosticon*, lib. iii: "We confess, that there is in all men a free will, which hath indeed the judgment of reason; not that it is thereby fitted, without God, either to begin or to perform anything in matters pertaining to God, but only in works belonging to this present life, whether they be good or evil. By good works, [5] I mean those which are of the goodness of nature; as to will to labor in the field, to desire meat or drink, to desire to have a friend, to desire apparel, to desire to build a house, to marry a wife, to nourish cattle, to learn the art of divers good things, to desire any good thing pertaining to this present life; all which are not without God's government, yea, [6] they are, and had their beginning from God and by God. Among evil things, I account such as these: [7] to will to worship an image; to will manslaughter, and such like."

[8] They condemn the Pelagians, and others, who teach, that by the powers of nature alone,

without the Spirit of God, we are able to love God above all things; also to perform the commandments of God, as touching the substance of our actions. [9] For although nature be able in some sort to do the external works (for it is able to withhold the hands from theft and murder), yet it cannot work the inward motions, such as the fear of God, trust in God, chastity, patience, and such like.

ARTICLE XIX

Of the Cause of Sin

Touching the cause of sin, they teach, that although God doth create and preserve nature, yet the cause of sin is the will of the wicked; to wit, of the devil, and ungodly men; which will, God not aiding, turns itself from God, as Christ says, "When he speaks a lie, he speaks of his own." John 8:44.

ARTICLE XX

Of Good Works

[1] Ours are falsely accused of forbidding good works. For their writings extant upon the Ten Commandments, [2] and others of the like argument, do bear witness, that they have to good purpose taught concerning every kind of life, and its duties; what kinds of life, and what works in every calling, do please God. Of which things, [3] preachers in former times taught little or nothing: only they urged certain childish and needless

works; as, keeping of holidays, set fasts, fraternities, pilgrimages, worshipping of saints, the use of rosaries, monkery, and such like things. [4] Whereof our adversaries having had warning, they do now unlearn them, and do not preach concerning these unprofitable works, as they were wont. [5] Besides, they begin now to make mention of faith, concerning which there was formerly a deep silence. [6] They teach that we are not justified by works alone, but they conjoin faith and works, and say we are justified by faith and works. [7] Which doctrine is more tolerable than the former one, and can afford more consolation than their old doctrine.

[8] Whereas, therefore, the doctrine of faith, which should be the chief one in the Church, hath been so long unknown, as all men must needs grant, that there was the deepest silence about the righteousness of faith in their sermons, and that the doctrine of works was usual in the Churches, for this cause our Divines did thus admonish the Churches:

[9] First, that our works cannot reconcile God, or deserve remission of sins, grace, and justification at his hands, but that these we obtain by faith only, when we believe that we are received into favor for Christ's sake; who alone is appointed the Mediator and Propitiatory, by whom the Father is reconciled. He, [10] therefore, that trusts by his works to merit grace, despises the merit and grace of Christ, and seeks by his own power, without Christ, to come unto the Father: whereas Christ hath said expressly of himself, "I am the way, the truth, and the life." John 14:6.

[11] This doctrine of faith is handled by Paul almost everywhere: "By grace ye are saved through faith, and that not of yourselves, it is the gift of God; not of works:" Ephes. 2:8, 9. [12] And lest any here should cavil, that we bring in a new-found interpretation, this whole cause is sustained by testimonies of the Fathers. [13] Augustine doth in many volumes defend grace, and the righteousness of faith, against the merit of works. [14] The like doth Ambrose teach in his book, *De Vocatione Gentium*, and elsewhere; for thus he says of the calling of the Gentiles: "The redemption made by the blood of Christ would be of small account, and the prerogative of man's works would not give place to the mercy of God, if the justification which is by grace were due to merits going before; so as it should not be the liberality of the giver, but the wages or hire of the laborer."

[15] This doctrine though it be contemned of the unskillful, yet godly and fearful consciences find by experience that it brings very great comfort: because that consciences cannot be quieted by any works, but by faith alone, when they believe assuredly, that they have a God who is propitiated for Christ's sake; as Paul teaches, "Being justified by faith, [16] we have peace with God:" Rom. 5:1. [17] This doctrine doth wholly belong to the conflict of a troubled conscience; and cannot be understood, but where the conscience hath felt that conflict. Wherefore, [18] all such as have had no experience thereof, and all that are profane men, who dream that Christian righteousness is naught else but a civil and

philosophical righteousness, are poor judges of this matter.

[19] Formerly, men's consciences were vexed with the doctrine of works; they did not hear any comfort out of the Gospel. [20] Whereupon conscience drove some into the desert, into Monasteries, hoping there to merit grace by a monastical life. [21] Others devised other works, whereby to merit grace, and to satisfy for sin. [22] There was very great need therefore to teach and renew this doctrine of faith in Christ; to the end that fearful consciences might not want comfort, but might know that grace, and forgiveness of sins, and justification, were received by faith in Christ.

[23] Another thing, which we teach men, is, that in this place the name of FAITH doth not only signify a knowledge of the history, which may be in the wicked, and in the Devil, but that it signifies a faith which believeth, not only the history, but also the effect of the history; to wit, the article of remission of sins; namely, that by Christ we have grace, righteousness, and remission of sins. Now, [24] he that knows that he has the Father merciful to him through Christ, this man knows God truly: he knows that God hath a care of him; he loves God, and calls upon him; in a word, he is not without God, as the Gentiles are. For the devils, and the wicked, [25] can never believe this article of the remission of sins: and therefore they hate God as their enemy; they call not upon him, they look for no good thing at his hands. After this manner doth Augustine admonish the reader touching the name of Faith, [26] and teaches, that this word Faith is taken in Scriptures, not for such

a knowledge as is in the wicked, but for a trust, which doth comfort and lift up disquieted minds.

[27] Moreover, ours teach, that it is necessary to do good works; not that we may trust that we deserve grace by them, but because it is the will of God that we should do them. [28] By faith alone is apprehended remission of sins and grace. [29] And because the Holy Spirit is received by faith, our hearts are now renewed, and so put on new affections, so that they are able to bring forth good works. [30] For thus says Ambrose, "Faith is the begetter of a good will, and of good actions." For man's powers, [31] without the Holy Spirit, are full of wicked affections, and are weaker than that they can do any good deed before God. Besides, they are in the Devil's power, [32] who drives men forward into diverse sins, into profane opinions, and into heinous crimes: [33] as was to be seen in the philosophers, who, as saying to live an honest life, could not attain unto it, but were defiled with many heinous crimes. Such is the weakness of man, [34] when he is without faith and the Holy Spirit, and hath no other guide but the natural powers of man.

[35] Hereby every man may see that this doctrine is not to be accused, as forbidding good works; but rather is much to be commended, because it shows after what sort we must do good works. [36] For without faith, the nature of man can by no means perform the works of the First or Second Table. [37] Without faith, it cannot call upon God, hope in God, bear the cross; but seeks help from man, and trusts in man's help. So it cometh to pass, [38] that all lusts and human

counsels bear sway in the heart so long as faith and trust in God is absent.

[39] Wherefore also Christ says, "Without me you can do nothing," John 15:5, and the Church sings, "Without thy power is naught in man, [40] naught that is innocent."

ARTICLE **XXI**

Of the Worship of Saints

[1] Touching the worship of saints, they teach, that the memory of saints may be set before us, that we may follow their faith and good works according to our calling; as the Emperor may follow David's example in making war to drive away the Turks from his country: for either of them is a king. [2] But the Scripture teaches not to invocate saints, or to ask help of saints, because it propounds unto us one Christ the Mediator, Propitiatory, High Priest, and Intercessor. [3] This Christ is to be invocated, and he hath promised that he will hear our prayers, and likes this worship especially, to wit, that he be invocated in all afflictions. "If any man sin, we have an advocate with God, Jesus Christ the righteous:" 1 John 2:1.

[4] This is about the sum of doctrine among us, in which can be seen that there is nothing which is discrepant with the Scriptures, or with the Church Catholic, or even with the Roman Church, so far as that Church is known from writers [the writings of the Fathers]. This being the case they judge us harshly, who insist that we shall be regarded as heretics. [5] But the dissension is concerning

certain [traditions and] abuses, which without any certain authority have crept into the Churches, in which things even if there were some difference, yet would it be a becoming lenity on the part of the bishops, that on account of the Confession which we have now presented, they should bear with us, since not even the Canons are so severe, as to demand the same rites everywhere, nor were the rites of all Churches at any time the same. [6] Although among us in large part the ancient rites are diligently observed. [7] For it is a calumnious falsehood, that all the ceremonies, all the things instituted of old are abolished in our Churches. But the public complaint was, [8] that certain abuses were connected with the rites in common use. These, because they could not with good conscience be approved, have to some extent been corrected.

II

ARTICLES IN WHICH ARE RECOUNTED THE ABUSES WHICH HAVE BEEN CORRECTED

[1] Inasmuch as the Churches among us, dissent in no article of faith from the Church Catholic [the Universal Christian Church], and only omit a few of certain abuses, which are novel [in part have crept in with time, in part have been introduced by violence], and contrary to the purport of the Canons have been received by the fault of the times, we beg that Your Imperial Majesty would clemently hear both what ought to be changed, and what are the reasons that the people ought not to be forced against their con sciences to observe those abuses. [2] Nor should Your Imperial Majesty have faith in those who, that they may inflame the hatred of men against us, scatter amazing slanders among the people. [3] In this way the minds of good men being angered at the beginning they gave occasion to this dissension, and by the same art they now endeavor to increase the discords. [4] For beyond doubt Your

Imperial Majesty will find that the form both of doctrines and of ceremonies among us, is far more tolerable than that which these wicked and malicious men describe. The truth, moreover, [5] cannot be gathered from common rumors and the reproaches of enemies. But it is easy to judge this, [6] that nothing is more profitable to preserve the dignity of ceremonies and to nurture reverence and piety among the people, than that the ceremonies should be rightly performed in the Churches.

ARTICLE **XXII.** (I.)

Of both Kinds [in the Lord's Supper]

[1] Both kinds of the Sacrament in the Lord's Supper are given to the laity, because that this custom hath the commandment of the Lord, "Drink all ye of this:" Matt. 26:27; where Christ doth manifestly command concerning the cup, that all should drink. [2] And that no man might cavil, that this doth only pertain to the priests, the example of Paul to the Corinthians witnesses, that the whole Church did use both kinds in common: 1 Cor. 11:28. [3] And this custom remained a long time in the Church; neither is it certain, when, or by what authority, it was changed. [4] Cyprian in certain places doth witness, that the blood was given to the people: the same thing doth Jerome testify, [5] saying, The priests do minister the Eucharist, and communicate the blood of Christ to the people." Nay, Pope Gelasius commanded, [6] that the Sacrament be not divided: *Dist. 2, De Consecr. Cap. Comperimus.* [7] Only a custom, [9] not thus

ancient, doth otherwise. [8] But it is manifest that a custom, [9] brought in contrary to the commandments of God, is not to be approved, as the Canons do witness: *Dist.* 8, *Cap. Veritate*; with the words which follow. [10] Now this custom has been received, not only against the Scripture, but also against the ancient Canons, and the example of the Church. [11] Therefore if any would rather use both kinds in the Sacrament, they are not to be compelled to do otherwise with the offence of their conscience. And because that the division of the Sacrament doth not agree with the institution of Christ, [12] among us it is the custom to omit that procession which hitherto hath been in use.

ARTICLE XXIII. (II.)

Of the Marriage of Priests

[1] There was a common complaint of the examples of such priests as were not continent. [2] For which cause also Pope Pius is reported to have said, "that there were certain causes for which marriage was forbidden to priests, but there were many weightier causes why it should be permitted again:" for so Platina writes. [3] Whereas therefore the priests among us seek to avoid these public offences, they have married wives, and have taught that it is lawful for them to enter into marriage. First, because that Paul says, [4] "To avoid fornication, let every man have his wife:" again, "It is better to marry than to burn:" 1 Cor. 7:2, 9. Secondly, Christ says, [5] "All men cannot receive this word:" Matt. 19:11; where he shows that all men are not fit for a single life, because that God

created mankind, male and female: Gen. 1:28. [6] Nor is it in man's power, without a special gift and work of God, to alter his creation. [7] Therefore such as are not meet for a single life, ought to contract marriage. [8] For no law of man, no vow, can take away the commandment of God, and his ordinance. [9] By these reasons the priests do prove that they may lawfully take wives. And it is well known, [10] that in the ancient Churches priests were married. For Paul says, [11] "that a bishop must be chosen which is a husband:" 1 Tim. 3:2. And in Germany, [12] not until about four hundred years ago, the priests were by violence compelled to live a single life; who then were so wholly bent against the matter, that the Archbishop of Mentz, being about to publish the Pope of Rome's decree to that effect, was almost murdered in a tumult by the priests in their anger. And the matter was handled so rudely, [13] that not only were marriages forbidden for the time to come, but also such as were then contracted, were broken asunder, contrary to all laws divine and human, contrary to the Canons themselves, that were before made not only by Popes, but also by most famous Councils. And seeing that, as the world decays, [14] man's nature by little and little waxes weaker, it is well to look to it, that no more vices do overspread Germany. Furthermore, [15] God ordained marriage to be a remedy for man's infirmity. [16] The Canons themselves do say, that the old rigor is now and then in latter times to be released because of the weakness of men. Which it were to be wished might be done in this matter also. [17] And if marriage be forbidden any longer, the Churches may at length want pastors.

[18] Seeing then that there is a plain commandment of God; seeing the use of the Church is well known; seeing that impure single life brings forth very many offences, adulteries, and other enormities worthy to be punished by the godly magistrate, it is a marvel that greater cruelty should be showed in no other thing, than against the marriage of priests. God hath commanded to honor marriage: [19] the laws in all well-ordered commonwealths, [20] even among the heathen, have adorned marriages with very great honors. But now men are cruelly put to death, yea, [21] and priests also, contrary to the mind of the Canons, for no other cause, but marriage. [22] Paul calls that "a doctrine of devils," which forbids marriage: 1 Tim. 4:1; which may now very well be seen, [23] since the forbidding of marriage is maintained by such punishments. [24] But as no law of man can take away the law of God, no more can any vow whatsoever. [25] Therefore Cyprian giveth counsel, that those women should marry, which do not keep their vowed chastity. His words are these, in the 1st Book, the 2d Epistle: "If they will not or are not able to endure, it is far better they should marry, than that they should fall into the fire by their importunate desires. In anywise let them give no offence to their brethren or sisters." Yea, [26] even the Canons show some kind of justice towards such as before their ripe years did vow chastity; as hitherto the use hath for the most part been.

ARTICLE **XXIV.** (III.)

Of the Mass

[1] Our Churches are wrongfully accused to have abolished the Mass. For the Mass is retained still among us, and celebrated with great reverence; yea, [2] and almost all the ceremonies that are in use, saving that with the things sung in Latin, we mingle certain things sung in German at various parts of the service, which be added for the people's instruction. For therefore alone we have need of ceremonies, [3] that they may teach the unlearned. [4] This is not only commanded by St. Paul, to use a tongue that the people understand, 1 Cor. 14:9, but man's law hath also appointed it. [5] We accustom the people to receive the Sacrament together, if so be any be found fit thereunto; and that is a thing that doth increase the reverence and due estimation of the public ceremonies. For none are admitted, [6] except they be first proved. Besides, [7] we put men in mind of the worthiness and use of the Sacrament, how great comfort it brings to fearful consciences; that they may learn to believe God, and to look for and crave all good things at his hands. This worship doth please God: [8] such an use of the Sacrament doth nourish piety towards God. [9] Therefore it seems not that Masses be more religiously celebrated among our adversaries, than with us.

[10] But it is evident, that of long time this hath been the public and most grievous complaint of all good men, that Masses are basely profaned, being used for gain. And it is not unknown, [11] how far this abuse hath spread itself in all

Churches; of what manner of men Masses are used, only for a reward, or for wages; and how many do use them against the prohibition of the Canons. [12] But Paul doth grievously threaten those who treat the Lord's Supper unworthily, saying, "He that eats this bread or drinks this cup of the Lord unworthily, shall be guilty of the body and blood of the Lord:" 1 Cor. 11:27. Therefore, [13] when the priests among us were admonished of this sin, private Masses were laid aside among us, seeing that for the most part there were no private Masses but only for lucre's sake. [14] Neither were the bishops ignorant of these abuses, and if they had amended them in time, there had now been less of dissensions. [15] Heretofore, by their dissembling, they suffered much corruption to creep into the Church: now they begin, [16] though it be late, to complain of the calamities of the Church; seeing that this tumult was raised up by no other mean, than by those abuses, which were so evident, that they could no longer be tolerated. [17] There were many dissensions, concerning the Mass, concerning the Sacrament. [18] And perhaps the world is punished for so long a profaning of Masses, which they, who both could and ought to have amended it, have so many years tolerated in the Churches. [19] For in the Ten Commandments it is written, "He that taketh in vain the name of the Lord, shall not be held guiltless:" Exod. 20:7. [20] And from the beginning of the world, there neither was nor is any divine thing, which seems so to have been employed for gain, as the Mass.

[21] There was added an opinion, which increased private Masses infinitely; to wit, that Christ by his passion did satisfy for original sin, and appointed the Mass, wherein an oblation should be made for daily sins, both mortal and venial. [22] Hereupon a common opinion was received, that the Mass is a work, that taketh away the sins of the quick and the dead, and that for the doing of the work. [23] Here men began to dispute, whether one Mass said for many were of as great force, as particular Masses said for particular men. This disputation hath brought forth that infinite multitude of Masses. [24] Our preachers have admonished, concerning these opinions, that they do depart from the holy Scriptures, and diminish the glory of the passion of Christ. [25] For the passion of Christ was an oblation and satisfaction, not only for original sin, but also for all other sins; as it is written in the Epistle to the Hebrews, 10:10: [26] "We are sanctified by the oblation of Jesus Christ once made:" also, [27] "By one oblation he hath perfected forever them that are sanctified:" Heb. 10:14. [28] The Scripture also teach, that we are justified before God through faith in Christ, when we believe that our sins are forgiven for Christ's sake. Now, [29] if the Mass do take away the sins of the quick and the dead, even for the work's sake that is done, then justification cometh by the work of Masses, and not by faith; which the Scripture cannot endure. [30] But Christ commands us "to do it in remembrance of himself:" Luke 22:19, therefore the Mass has been instituted, that faith, in them which use the Sacrament, may remember what benefits it receives by Christ, and

that it may raise and comfort the fearful conscience. [31] For this is to remember Christ, to wit, to remember his benefits, and to feel and perceive that they be indeed imparted unto us. [32] Nor is it sufficient to call to mind the history; because that the Jews also, and the wicked, can do. [33] Therefore the Mass must be used to this end, that there the Sacrament may be reached unto them that have need of comfort; as Ambrose said, "Because I do always sin, therefore I ought always to receive the medicine." [34] And seeing that the Mass is such a communion of the Sacrament, we do observe one common Mass every holyday, and on other days, if any will use the Sacrament, at which times it is offered to them which desire it. [35] Neither is this custom newly brought into the Church. For the ancients, before Gregory's time, make no mention of any private Mass: of the common Mass they speak much. Chrysostom said, [36] "that the priest doth daily stand at the altar, and call some unto the Communion, and put back others." [37] And by the ancient Canons it is evident that someone did celebrate the Mass, of whom the other elders and deacons did receive the body of the Lord. [38] For so the words of the Nicene Canon do sound: "Let the deacons in their order, after the elders, receive the holy Communion of a bishop, or of an elder." And Paul, [39] concerning the Communion, commands, "that one tarry for another," 1 Cor. 11:33, that so there may be a common participation. [40] Seeing therefore that the Mass amongst us hath the example of the Church, out of the Scripture, and the Fathers, we trust that it cannot be disapproved;

especially since our public ceremonies are kept, the most part, like unto the usual ceremonies: only the number of Masses is not alike, the which, by reason of very great and manifest abuses, it were certainly far better to be moderated. For in times past also, [41] in the Churches whereunto was greatest resort, it was not the use to have Mass said every day; as the Tripartite History, *lib.* 9, *cap.* 38, doth witness. "Again," said it, "in Alexandria, every fourth and sixth day of the week, the Scriptures are read, and the doctors do interpret them: and all other things are done also, except only the celebration of the Eucharist."

ARTICLE XXV. (IV.)

Of Confession

[1] Confession is not abolished in our Churches. For it is not usual to communicate the body of our Lord, except to those who have been previously examined and absolved. [2] And the people are taught most carefully concerning the faith required to absolution, about which before these times there has been a deep silence. Men are taught, [3] that they should highly regard absolution, inasmuch as it is God's voice, and pronounced by God's command.

[4] The power of the keys is honored, and mention is made, how great consolation it brings to terrified consciences, and that God requires faith, that we believe that absolution as a voice sounding from heaven, and that this faith in Christ truly obtains and receives remission of sins.

[5] Aforetime satisfactions were immoderately extolled: of faith, and the merit of Christ, and justification by faith no mention was made. Wherefore on this point our Churches are by no means to be blamed. For this even our adversaries are compelled to concede in regard to us, [6] that the doctrine of repentance is most diligently treated and laid open by us.

[7] But of Confession our Churches teach, that the enumeration of sins is not necessary, nor are consciences to be burdened with the care of enumerating" all sins, inasmuch as it is impossible to recount all sins, as the Psalm (19:13) testifies: [8] "Who can understand his errors?" So also Jeremiah (17:9): "The heart is deceitful above all things, and desperately wicked. Who can know it?" [9] But if no sins were remitted except what were recounted, consciences could never find peace, because very many sins they can neither see nor remember.

[10] The ancient writers also testify that the enumeration is not necessary. [11] For in the Decrees Chrysostom is cited, who speaks thus: "I do not say to thee, that you should discover yourself in public, or accuse yourself before others, but I would have thee obey the prophet when he says: 'Reveal thy way unto the Lord.' Therefore with prayer confess thy sins before God the true Judge. Pronounce thine errors, not with the tongue, but with the memory of thy conscience." And the Gloss (*Of Repentance*, [12] Dist. V, Chap. *Consideret*), admits that Confession is of human right only [is not commanded in Scripture, but has been instituted by the Church].

[13] Nevertheless, on account of the very great benefit of absolution, as well as for other uses to the conscience, Confession is retained among us.

ARTICLE XXVI. (V.)

Of the Distinction of Meats, and of Traditions

[1] It hath been a general opinion, not of the people alone, but also of such as are teachers in the Churches, that the differences of meats, and such like human traditions, are works available to merit grace, and are satisfactions for sins. [2] And that the world thus thought is apparent by this; that daily new ceremonies, new orders, new holidays, new fasts, were appointed: and the teachers in the Churches did exact these works as a service necessary to deserve grace; and they did greatly terrify men's consciences, if aught were omitted.

Of this persuasion concerning traditions, [3] many disadvantages have followed in the Church. [4] For first the doctrine of grace is obscured by it, and also the righteousness of faith, which is the principal part of the Gospel, and which it behooves most of all to stand forth and to have the pre-eminence in the Church, that the merit of Christ may be well known, and faith, which believeth that sins are remitted for Christ's sake, may be exalted far above works. [5] For which cause also Paul lays much stress on this point: he removes the law, and human traditions, that he may show that the righteousness of Christ is a far other thing, than such works as these be, namely, a faith, which believeth that sins are freely remitted for Christ's sake. [6] But this doctrine of Paul is almost wholly

smothered by traditions, which have bred an
opinion, that, by making difference in meats, and
such like services, a man should merit grace and
justification. [7] In their doctrine of repentance
there was no mention of faith; only these works of
satisfaction were spoken of: repentance seemed to
consist wholly in these.

[8] Secondly, these traditions obscured the
commandments of God, because traditions were
preferred far above the commandments of God. All
Christianity was thought to be an observation of
certain holidays, rites, fasts, and attire. [9] These
observations were in possession of a most goodly
title, that they were the spiritual life, and the
perfect life. In the meantime, [10] God's
commandments, touching every man's calling,
were of small estimation: that the father brought
up his children, that the mother nurtured them,
that the prince governed the commonwealth.
These were reputed worldly affairs, and imperfect,
and far inferior to those glittering observances.
[11] And this error did greatly torment pious
consciences, which were grieved that they were
held by an imperfect kind of life, in marriage, in
magistracy, or in other civil functions. They had
the monks, and such like, in admiration, and
falsely imagined that the observances of these men
were more grateful to God than their own.

[12] Thirdly, traditions brought great danger to
men's consciences, because it was impossible to
keep all traditions, and yet men thought the
observation of them to be necessary services.
Gerson writes, [13] "that many fell into despair,
and some murdered themselves, because they

perceived that they could not keep the traditions:" and all this while, they never heard the comfort of the righteousness of faith, or of grace. [14] We see the Summists and divines gather together the traditions, and seek qualifications of them, to unburden men's consciences: and yet all will not serve, but meantime they bring more snares upon the conscience. [15] The schools and pulpits have been so busied in gathering together the traditions, that they had not leisure to touch the Scripture, and to seek out a more profitable doctrine, of faith, of the cross, of hope, of the dignity of civil affairs, of the comfort of conscience in arduous trials. Wherefore Gerson, [16] and some other divines, have made grievous complaints, that they were hindered by these arguments about traditions, so that they could not be occupied in some better kind of doctrine. [17] And Augustine forbids that men's consciences should be burdened with observations of this kind, and doth very prudently warn Januarius to know, that they are to be observed as things indifferent; for he so speaks. Wherefore our ministers must not be thought to have touched this matter rashly, [18] or from hatred of the bishops, as some do falsely surmise. [19] There was great need to admonish the Churches of those errors, which did arise from mistaking of traditions: [20] for the Gospel compels men to urge the doctrine of grace, and of the righteousness of faith, in the Church; which yet can never be understood, if men suppose that they can merit remission of sins, and justification, by observances of their own choice. [21] Thus therefore they teach us, that we cannot merit grace, or justification, by the observation of man's traditions; and therefore we must not think that such observations are necessary service. [22] Hereunto they add testimonies out of the Scriptures. Christ excuses his disciples, which kept not the received tradition (which yet seemed to be about a matter not unlawful, but indifferent, and to have some affinity with the baptisms of the law); and says, "They worship me in vain with the commandments of men:" Matt. 15:9. [23] Christ therefore exacts no unprofitable service. And a little after, he adds: "Whatsoever enters in at the mouth defiles not the man:" ver. 11. [24] So also Paul: "The kingdom of God is not meat and drink:" Rom. 15:17. [25] "Let no man judge you in meat or drink, or in respect of the Sabbath-days, or of a holiday:" Col. 2:16. Again: [26] "If ye be dead with Christ from the rudiments of the world, why, as though ye lived in the world, are ye subject to traditions; Touch not, taste not, handle not?" ver. 20, 21. Peter says, [27] "Why tempt ye God, laying a yoke upon the necks of the disciples, which neither we, nor our fathers, were able to bear? But we believe that through the grace of the Lord Jesus Christ, we shall be saved, even as they:" Acts 15:10, 11. [28] Here Peter forbids to burden the consciences with many rites, whether they be of Moses', or of any others', appointing. And Paul calls the forbidding of meats, [29] "a doctrine of devils:" 1 Tim. 4:1, because that it is against the Gospel, to appoint or do such works, to the end that by them we may merit grace, or justification, or as though Christianity could not exist without such service.

[30] Here our adversaries object against us, that our ministers hinder all good discipline, and mortification of the flesh; as Jovinian did. But the contrary may be seen by our men's writings. [31] For they have always taught, touching the cross, that Christians ought to bear afflictions. This is the true, earnest, [32] and unfeigned mortification, to be exercised with divers afflictions, and to be crucified with Christ. Moreover they teach, [33] that every Christian must so by bodily discipline, or bodily exercises and labor, exercise and keep himself under, that plenty and sloth do not stimulate him to sin; not that he may by such exercises merit grace, or satisfy for sins. And this corporal discipline should be used always, [34] not only on a few, and set days; according to the commandment of Christ: [35] "Take heed lest your hearts be overcharged with surfeiting:" Luke 21:34. Again, [36] "This kind (of devils) goes not out but by prayer and fasting:" Matt. 17:21. And Paul says, "I keep under my body, [37] and bring it into subjection:" 1 Cor. 9:27, where he plainly shows, [38] that he did therefore chastise his body, not that by that discipline he might merit remission of sins, but that his body might be apt and fit for spiritual things and to do his duty, according to his calling. Therefore we do not condemn fasts themselves, [39] but the traditions which prescribe certain days and certain meats, with danger to the conscience, as though such works as these were a necessary service.

[40] Yet most of the traditions are observed among us, which tend unto this end, that things may be done orderly in the Church; as namely, the

order of Lessons in the Mass, and the chiefest holidays. But, [41] in the meantime, men are admonished, that such a service doth not justify before God, and that it is not to be supposed there is sin in such things, if they be left undone, without scandal. [42] This liberty in human rites and ceremonies was not unknown to the Fathers. [43] For in the East they kept Easter at another time than they did in Rome: and when they of Rome accused the East of schism for this diversity, they were admonished by others, that such customs need not be alike everywhere. And Irenaeus says: [44] "The disagreement about fasting doth not break off the agreement of faith." Besides, Pope Gregory, in the 12th Distinction, intimates, that such diversity doth not hurt the unity of the Church: [45] and in the *Tripartite History, lib.* 9, many examples of dissimilar rites are gathered together, and these words are there rehearsed, "The mind of the Apostles was, not to give precepts concerning holidays, but to preach godliness and a holy life [faith and love]."

ARTICLE XXVII. (VI.)

Of Monastic Vows

[1] What is taught amongst us touching the Vows of Monks will be better understood, if one call to mind what was the state of monasteries, and how many things were every day committed in the monasteries, contrary to the Canons. In Augustine's time, [2] cloister-fraternities were free; but afterward, when discipline was corrupted, vows were everywhere laid upon them, that, as it

were in a newly-devised prison, the discipline might be restored again. Over and besides vows, [3] many other observances by little and little were added. [4] And these bands and snares were cast upon many, before they came to ripe years, contrary to the Canons. [5] Many through error fell into this kind of life unawares, who, though they wanted not years, yet they wanted discretion to judge of their strength and ability. [6] They who were once got within these nets, were constrained to abide in them, though, by the benefit of the Canons, some might be set at liberty. [7] And that fell out rather in the monasteries of nuns than of monks; although the weaker sex ought more to have been spared. [8] This rigor and severity displeased many good men heretofore, when they saw young maids and young men thrust into monasteries, there to get their living. They saw what an unhappy issue this counsel had, what offences it bred, and what snares it laid upon consciences. [9] They were grieved that the authority of the Canons was wholly neglected and contemned in a thing most dangerous. [10] To all these evils there was added such a persuasion concerning vows, as, it is well known, did in former times, displease the monks themselves, if any of them were somewhat wiser than the rest. [11] They taught that vows were equal to baptism: they taught that by this kind of life they merited remission of sins, and justification before God; yea, they added, [12] that the monk's life did not only merit righteousness before God, but more than that, because it observed, not only the commandments, but also the counsels of the

Gospel. And thus they taught, [13] that the monk's profession was better than baptism, that the monk's life did merit more than the life of magistrates, of pastors, and such like, who, in obedience to God's commandment, followed their calling, without any such religions of man's making. [14] None of these things can be denied: they are to be seen in their writings. What occurred afterward in the monasteries? [15] In old time they were schools for the study of sacred letters, and other branches of knowledge, which were profitable to the Church; and thence were pastors and bishops taken: but now the case is altered. It is needless to rehearse what is notorious. [16] In old time they came together into such places to learn: but now they feign that it is a kind of life taken up to merit remission of sins, and justification; yea, they say, it is a state of perfection, and prefer it to all other kinds of life, the kinds that God ordained. We have therefore mentioned these things, [17] not to excite odium, exaggerating nothing, to the end that the doctrine of our Churches touching this matter might be understood.

[18] First, concerning such as contract marriage, thus they teach among us: that it is lawful for any to marry, that are not adapted for a single life; forasmuch as vows cannot take away God's ordinance and commandment. The commandment of God is, [19] "To avoid fornication, let every man have his own wife:" 1 Cor. 7:2. And not only the commandment, [20] but also the creation and ordinance of God, compels such unto marriage, as without the special work of

God are not exempted; according to that saying, "It is not good for man to be alone:" Gen. 2:18. [21] They therefore that are obedient to this commandment and ordinance of God, do not sin.

[22] What can be said against these things? Let a man exaggerate the bond of a vow as much as he will, yet can he never bring to pass that the vow shall take away God's commandment. The Canons teach, [23] "that in every vow the right of the superior is excepted:" much less therefore can these vows, which are contrary to God's commandment, be of force.

[24] If so be that the obligation of vows has no cause why it might be changed, then could not the Roman Pontiffs have dispensed therewith. For neither is it lawful for man to disannul that bond, which doth simply belong to the law of God. [25] But the Roman Pontiffs have judged very prudently, that in this obligation there must equity be used: therefore they often, as we read, have dispensed with vows. [26] The history of the King of Arragon, being called back out of a monastery, is well known; and there are examples in our own time.

[27] Secondly, why do our adversaries exaggerate the obligation, or the effect of the vow; when in the meantime they speak not a word of the very nature of a vow, that it ought to be in a thing possible, ought to be voluntary, and taken up of a man's own accord, and with deliberation? But it is not unknown, [28] how far perpetual chastity is in the power of a man. And how many a one amongst them is there, that doth vow of his own accord, and well advised? [29] Maidens and

youths, before they know how to judge, are persuaded, yea, sometimes also compelled, to vow. [30] Wherefore it is not meet to dispute so rigorously of the obligation, seeing that all men confess, that it is against the nature of a vow, that it is not done of a man's own accord, nor advisedly.

[31] The Canons for the most part disannul vows, which are made before fifteen years of age; because that, before one come to that age, there seems not to be so much judgment, that determination may be made concerning a perpetual life. Another Canon, [32] permitting more to the weakness of men, doth add some years more; for it forbids a vow to be made, before one be eighteen years of age. [33] But which of these shall we follow? The greatest part have this excuse for forsaking monasteries, because most of them vowed before they came to this age.

[34] Last of all, even though the breaking of a vow were to be reprehended, yet it seems not to follow directly that the marriages of such persons are to be dissolved. For Augustine, in his 27th quest. 1st chapt. [35] *Of Marriages*, doth deny that they ought to be dissolved: and his authority is not lightly to be esteemed, although others afterward have thought otherwise. [36] And although the commandment of God, touching wedlock, doth free most men from vows; yet our teachers do also bring another reason concerning vows, to show that they are void: because that all the worship of God, instituted of men without the commandment of God, and chosen to merit remission of sins, and justification, is wicked; as Christ says: "In vain

they do worship me, teaching for doctrines the commandments of men:" Matt. 15:9. [37] And Paul doth everywhere teach, that righteousness is not to be sought of our own observances, and services which are devised by men; but that it cometh by faith to those that believe that they are received into favor by God for Christ's sake. [38] But it is evident that the monks did teach, that these counterfeited religions satisfy for sins, and merit grace and justification. What else is this, than to detract from the glory of Christ, and to obscure and deny the righteousness of faith? Wherefore it follows, [39] that these common vows were wicked services, and are therefore void. For a wicked vow, [40] and that which is made against the commandments of God, is one of no force; neither, as the Canon said, ought a vow to be a bond of iniquity. Paul says, "Christ is become of no effect unto you, [41] whosoever of you are justified by the law; ye are fallen from grace:" Gal. 5:4. [42] They therefore who wish to be justified by vows, are made void of Christ, and fall from grace. [43] For they also who attribute justification to their vows, attribute to their own works what properly belongs to the glory of Christ. Nor truly can it be denied, [44] that the monks taught that they are justified by their vows and observances, and merit the remission of sins; nay, they invented yet greater absurdities, and said they could transfer their good works to others. [45] If any man wished to expand these things, so as to excite odium, how many things might he rehearse, whereof the monks themselves are now ashamed! Moreover, [46] they would persuade men that these invented religious orders are a state of Christian perfection. [47] Or is this not attributing justification to works? [48] It is no light offence in the Church to propound unto the people a certain service devised by men, without the commandment of God, and to teach that such a service doth justify men: because that the righteousness of faith, which ought especially to be taught in the Church, is obscured, when those marvelous religions of angels, the pretense of poverty and humility, and of celibacy, are cast before men's eyes. Moreover the commandments of God, [49] and the true worship of God, are obscured, when men hear that monks alone are in that state of perfection: because that Christian perfection is this, to fear God sincerely, and again, to conceive great faith, and to trust assuredly that God is pacified toward us, for Christ's sake; to ask, and certainly to look for, help from God in all our affairs, according to our calling; and outwardly to do good works diligently, and to attend to our vocation. [50] In these things doth true perfection and the true worship of God consist: it doth not consist in singleness of life, in beggary, or in vile apparel.

[51] The people also conceive many pernicious opinions from these false commendations of the monastic life. They hear celibacy praised above measure: [52] therefore with offence of conscience they live in marriage. They hear that mendicants only are perfect; [53] therefore with offence of conscience they keep their possessions, and buy and sell. [54] They hear that the Gospel only giveth counsel not to take revenge: therefore some in private life are not afraid to avenge themselves;

for they hear that it is a counsel, not a commandment. [55] Others do think that all magistracy and civil offices are unworthy a Christian man. We read examples of men, who, [56] forsaking wedlock, and leaving the government of the common wealth, have hid themselves in monasteries. [57] This they called flying out of the world, and seeking a kind of life which is more acceptable to God: neither did they see that God is to be served in those commandments which he himself hath delivered, not in the commandments which are devised by men. [58] That is a good and perfect kind of life, which hath the commandment of God for it. [59] It is necessary to admonish men of these things. [60] And before these times Gerson did reprehend this error of the monks concerning perfection; and witnesses, that in his time this was a new saying, that the monastic life is a state of perfection. [61] Thus many wicked opinions do cleave fast unto vows: as that they merit remission of sins and justification, that they are Christian perfection, that they do keep the counsels and commandments, that they have works of supererogation. [62] All these things (seeing they be false and vain) do make vows to be of none effect.

Article XXVIII. (VII.)

Of Ecclesiastical Power

[1] There have been great controversies touching the power of bishops; in which many have incommodiously mingled together the

Ecclesiastical power, and the power of the sword. [2] And out of this confusion there have sprung very great wars and tumults, while that the Pontiffs trusting in the power of the keys, have not only appointed new kinds of service, and burdened men's consciences by reserving of cases, and by violent excommunications; but have also endeavored to transfer worldly kingdoms from one to another, and to despoil emperors of their power and authority. [3] These faults did godly and learned men long since reprehend in the Church; [4] and for that cause, our teachers were compelled, for the comfort of men's consciences, to show the difference between the Ecclesiastical power and the power of the sword. And they have taught that both of them, because of God's commandment, are dutifully to be reverenced and honored, as the greatest blessings of God upon earth.

[5] Now, their judgment is this: that the power of the keys, or the power of the bishops, by the rule of the Gospel, is a power, or commandment from God, of preaching the Gospel, of remitting or retaining sins, and of administering the Sacraments. [6] For Christ doth send his Apostles with this charge: "As the Father hath sent me, even so send I you. Receive the Holy Ghost: whosoever sins ye remit, they are remitted unto them; and whosoever sins ye retain, they are retained:" John 20:21–23. "Go, [7] and preach the Gospel to every creature," & c.: Mark 16:15. This power is put in execution, [8] only by teaching or preaching the Gospel, and administering the Sacraments, either to many, or to single

individuals, in accordance with their call. [9] For thereby not corporal things, but eternal, are granted; as an eternal righteousness, the Holy Ghost, life everlasting. [10] These things cannot be got, but by the ministry of the word and of the Sacraments: as Paul says, "The Gospel is the power of God to salvation to everyone that believeth:" Rom. 1:16. [11] Seeing then that the Ecclesiastical power concerns things eternal, and is exercised only by the ministry of the word, it hinders not the political government, any more than the art of singing hinders political government. [12] For the political administration is occupied about other matters than is the Gospel. The magistracy defends not the minds, but the bodies, and bodily things, against manifest injuries; and coerces men by the sword and corporal punishments, that it may uphold civil justice and peace.

[13] Wherefore the Ecclesiastical and civil powers are not to be confounded. The Ecclesiastical power hath its own commandment to preach the Gospel, and administer the Sacraments. [14] Let it not by force enter into the office of another; let it not transfer worldly kingdoms; let it not abrogate the magistrates' laws; let it not withdraw from them lawful obedience; let it not hinder judgments touching any civil ordinances or contracts; let it not prescribe laws to the magistrate, touching the form of the republic; as Christ says, "My kingdom is not of this world:" [15] John 18:36. Again, [16] "Who made me a judge or a divider over you?" Luke 12:14. And Paul says, [17] "Our conversation [citizenship] is in heaven:" Phil. 3:20. "The weapons of our warfare are not

carnal, but mighty through God, casting down imaginations," & c.: 2 Cor. 10:4. [18] In this way do our teachers distinguish between the duties of each power one from the other, and do warn all men to honor both powers, and to acknowledge both to be the [highest] gift and blessing of God.

[19] If so be that the bishops have any power of the sword, they have it not as bishops by the commandment of the Gospel, but by man's law given unto them of kings and emperors, for the civil government of their goods. This, however, is a kind of function diverse from the ministry of the Gospel.

[20] Therefore, when the question touches the jurisdiction of bishops, government must be distinguished from Ecclesiastical jurisdiction. Again, [21] by the Gospel, or, as they term it, by divine right, bishops, as bishops, that is, those who have the administration of the word and Sacraments committed to them, have no other jurisdiction at all, but only to remit sin, also to take cognizance of [to judge in regard to] doctrine, and to reject doctrine inconsistent with the Gospel, and to exclude from the communion of the Church, without human force, but by the word [of God], those whose wickedness is known. [22] And herein of necessity the Churches ought by Divine right to render obedience unto them; according to the saying of Christ, "He that hears you, hears me:" Luke 10:16. [23] But when they teach or determine anything contrary to the Gospel, then have the Churches a commandment of God, which forbids obedience to them: "Beware of false prophets:" Matt. 7:15. "If an angel from heaven preach any

other Gospel, [24] let him be accursed:" Gal. 1:9.
[25] "We cannot do anything against the truth, but
for the truth:" 2 Cor. 13:8. Also, "This power is
given us to edify, [26] and not to destroy:" 2 Cor.
13:10. [27] So do the Canons command; ii, *quæt* 7,
Cap. Sacerdotes; and *Cap. Oves.* And Augustine,
[28] in his *Treatise against Petilian's Epistle*, says,
"Neither must we subscribe to Catholic bishops, if
they chance to err, or determine anything contrary
to the canonical Scriptures."

[29] If so be that they have any other power or
jurisdiction, in hearing and understanding certain
cases, as namely, of Matrimony, and Tithes, & c.,
they hold it by human right. But when the
ordinaries fail [to attend to this office], princes are
constrained, whether they wish to do so or not, to
declare the law to their subjects, for maintaining of
peace.

[30] Besides these things, there is a
controversy, whether bishops or pastors have
power to institute ceremonies in the Church, and
to make laws concerning meats, and holidays, and
degrees, or orders of ministers. They that ascribe
this power to the bishops, [31] allege this
testimony for it: "I have yet many things to say
unto you, but ye cannot bear them now; but when
that Spirit of truth shall come, he shall teach you
all truth:" John 16:12, 13. [32] They allege also the
examples of the Apostles, who commanded to
abstain from blood, and that which was strangled:
Acts 15:29. They allege the change of the Sabbath
into the Lord's day, [33] contrary, as it seems, to
the Decalogue; and they have no example more in
their mouths, than the change of the Sabbath. They

will needs have the Church's power to be very great, because it hath dispensed with a precept of the Decalogue.

[34] But of this question ours do thus teach: that the bishops have no power to ordain anything contrary to the Gospel, as was showed before. The same also do the Canons teach, *Distinct.* 9. [35] Moreover it is against the Scripture, to ordain or require the observation of any traditions, to the end that we may merit remission of sins, and satisfy for sins by them. For the glory of Christ's merit suffers, [36] when we seek by such observances to merit justification. [37] And it is very apparent, that through this persuasion traditions grew into an infinite number in the Church. In the meanwhile, the doctrine concerning faith, and the righteousness of faith, was quite suppressed, for thereupon there were new holidays made, new fasts appointed, new ceremonies, new worships for saints, instituted; because that the authors of such things supposed by these works to merit grace. [38] After the same manner heretofore did the Penitential Canons increase, whereof we still see some traces in satisfactions.

[39] Moreover the authors of traditions do contrary to the command of God, when they find matters of sin in foods, in days and like things, and burden the Church with the servitude of the law, as if there ought to be among Christians, in order to merit justification, a service like the Levitical, the ordination of which God has committed to the Apostles and bishops. For this some of them write, [40] and the Pontiffs in some measure seem to be misled by the example of the Law of Moses. From

hence are those burdens, [41] that it is mortal sin, even without offence to others, to do manual labor on the festivals, that it is a mortal sin to omit the Canonical Hours, that certain foods defile the conscience, that fastings are works which appease God; that sin, in a reserved case, cannot be pardoned, but by the authority of him that reserved it; whereas the Canons speak only of reserving of Ecclesiastical penalty, and not of the reserving of the fault. Whence, then, [42] have the bishops power and authority of imposing these traditions upon the Churches, for the ensnaring of men's consciences, when Peter forbids (Acts 15:10) "to put a yoke upon the neck of the disciples," and St. Paul says (2 Cor. 13:10) that the power given him was to edification, not to destruction? Why, therefore, do they increase sins by these traditions? [43] For there are divers clear testimonies, which prohibit the making of such traditions, either to merit grace, or as things necessary to salvation. Paul says to the Colossians, [44] "Let no man judge you in meat, or in drink, or in respect of an holiday, or of the new moon, or of the Sabbath days:" Col. 2:16. Again, [45] "If ye be dead with Christ from the rudiments of the world, why, as though living in the world, are ye subject to ordinances (Touch not, taste not, handle not? which all are to perish with the using), after the commandments and doctrines of men? which things indeed have a show of wisdom:" Col. 2:20–23. [46] And to Titus he doth plainly forbid traditions: for he says, "Not giving heed to Jewish fables, and to commandments of men, that turn from the truth:" Tit. 1:14. [47] And Christ says of them, which urge traditions, "Let them alone; they be blind leaders of the blind:" Matt. 15:14. And he condemns such services: [48] "Every plant which my heavenly Father hath not planted, shall be rooted up:" ver. 13. [49] If bishops have authority to burden the Churches with innumerable traditions, and to snare men's consciences, why doth the Scripture so oft forbid to make and to listen to traditions? Why doth it call them the doctrines of devils? 1 Tim. 4:1. Hath the Holy Ghost warned us of them to no purpose?

[50] It remains, then, that (seeing ordinations, constituted as necessary, or with the opinion of meriting grace, are repugnant to the Gospel) it is not lawful for any bishops to institute or exact such worship. [51] For it is necessary that the doctrine of Christian liberty should be maintained in the Churches [Christendom]; that the bondage of the law is not necessary unto justification, as it is written to the Galatians, "Be not entangled again with the yoke of bondage:" Gal. 5:1. [52] It is necessary that the chiefest point of all the Gospel should be held fast, that we do freely obtain grace, by faith in Christ, not because of certain observances, or of services devised by men.

[53] What is then to be thought of the Lord's day, and of like rites of temples? Hereunto they [ours] answer, that it is lawful for bishops or pastors to make ordinances; whereby things may be done in order in the Church; not that by them we may merit grace, or satisfy for sins, or that men's consciences should be bound to esteem them as necessary services, and think that they sin when they violate them, without the offence of others. So

Paul ordained, [54] "that women should cover their heads in the congregation:" 1 Cor. 11:6; "that the interpreters of Scripture should be heard in order, in the Church:" 1 Cor. 14:27.

[55] Such ordinances it behooves the Churches to keep for charity and quietness' sake, so that one offend not another, that all things may be done in order, and without tumult in the Church, 1 Cor. 14:40, and Phil. 2:14, but so that consciences be not burdened, [56] so as to account them as things necessary to salvation, and think they sin when they violate them, without offence of others: as no one would say that a woman sins, if she went into public with her head uncovered, provided it were without the offence of men.

[57] Such is the observation of the Lord's day, of Easter, of Pentecost, and like holidays and rites. [58] For they that think that the observation of the Lord's day was appointed by the authority of the Church, instead of the Sabbath, as necessary, are greatly deceived. The Scripture, [59] which teach that all the Mosaic ceremonies can be omitted after the Gospel is revealed, has abrogated the Sabbath. And yet, [60] because it was requisite to appoint a certain day, that the people might know when they ought to come together, it appears that the [Christian] Church did for that purpose appoint the Lord's day: which for this cause also seemed to have been pleasing, that men might have an example of Christian liberty, and might know that the observation, neither of the Sabbath, nor of another day, was of necessity.

[61] There are certain marvelous disputations touching the changing of the law, and the

ceremonies of the new law, and the change of the Sabbath: which all arose from the false persuasion, that there should be a service in the Church, like to the Levitical; and that Christ committed to the Apostles and bishops, the devising new ceremonies, which should be necessary to salvation. These errors crept into the Church, [62] when the righteousness of faith was not plainly enough taught. Some dispute, [63] that the observation of the Lord's day is not indeed of the law of God, but *as it were* of the law of God: and touching holidays, they prescribe how far it is lawful to work in them. [64] What else are such disputations, but snares for men's consciences? For though they seek to moderate traditions, yet the equity of them can never be perceived, so long as the opinion of necessity remains; which must needs remain, where the righteousness of faith, and Christian liberty are not known.

[65] The Apostles commanded to abstain from blood: Acts 15:29. Who observes that nowadays? And yet they do not sin, that observe it not. For the Apostles themselves would not burden men's consciences with such a servitude: but they forbade it for a time, because of scandal. For in the decree, [66] the will of the Gospel is always to be considered. [67] Scarcely any Canons are precisely kept; and many grow out of use daily, yea, even among them that do most busily defend traditions. [68] Neither can there be sufficient care had of men's consciences, except this equity be kept, that men should know that such rites are not to be observed with any opinion of necessity, and that

men's consciences are not hurt, though traditions grow out of use.

[69] The bishops might easily retain lawful obedience, if they would not urge men to observe such traditions as cannot be kept with a good conscience. [70] Now they command single life; and they admit none, except they will swear not to teach the pure doctrine of the Gospel. The Churches do not desire of the bishops, [71] that they would repair peace and concord with the loss of their honor (which yet good pastors ought to do): [72] they only desire that they would remit unjust burdens, which are both new, and received contrary to the custom of the Catholic [Christian Universal] Church. It may well be, [73] that some constitutions had some probable reasons, when they began, which yet will not agree to latter times. It is evident, [74] that some were received through error. Wherefore it were a matter for the pontifical gentleness to mitigate them now; for such a change would not overthrow the unity of the Church. For many human traditions have been changed in time, as the Canons themselves declare. But if it cannot be obtained, [75] that those observances may be relaxed, which cannot be kept without sin, then must we follow the Apostles' rule, which wills "to obey God rather than men:" Acts 5:29. [76] Peter forbids bishops to be lords, and to be imperious over the Churches: 1 Pet. 5:3. [77] Now our meaning is not to have rule taken from the bishops: but this one thing only is requested at their hands, that they would suffer the Gospel to be purely taught, and that they would relax a few observances, which cannot be held

without sin. But if they will remit none, let them look how they will give account to God for this, that by their obstinacy they afford cause of schism.

CONCLUSION

[1] These are the principal articles which seem to be matters of controversy. For although we might speak of more abuses, yet that we may avoid undue length, we have embraced a few, whereby it is easy to judge of the others. [2] Great have been the complaints about indulgences, about pilgrimages, about the abuse of excommunication. The Parishes have been vexed in manifold ways by the stationary. Endless contentions have arisen between the pastors and the monks about parochial law, about confession, about burials, about sermons on extraordinary occasions, and about other things without number. [3] Things of this sort we pass over, that those which are chief in this matter being briefly set forth may more easily be noted. [4] Nor has anything been here said or adduced for the purpose of casting reproach on any one. Those things also have been enumerated, [5] which it seemed necessary to say, that it might be understood, that in doctrine and ceremonials among us there is nothing received contrary to Scripture or to the Catholic [Universal Christian] Church, inasmuch as it is manifest that we have diligently taken heed that no new and godless doctrines should creep into our Churches.

[6] In accordance with the Edict of His Imperial Majesty, we wish to present these articles above written, in which is our Confession, and in which

is seen a summary of the doctrine of those who teach among us. If anything be lacking in this Confession, [7] we are prepared, God willing, to present ampler information, in accordance with the Scriptures.

[8] Your Imperial Majesty's
most faithful and humble,

[9] JOHN, Duke of Saxony, Elector.

[10] GEORGE, Margrave of Brandenburg.

[11] ERNEST, Duke of Luneburg.

[12] PHILIP, Landgrave of Hesse.

[13] JOHN FREDERICK, Duke of Saxony.

[14] FRANCIS, Duke of Luneburg.

[15] WOLFGANG, Prince of Anhalt.

[16] SENATE and MAGISTRACY of Nurenberg.

[17] SENATE of Reutlingen.

NOTES

ON SOME PARTS OF THE AUGSBURG CONFESSION WHICH HAVE BEEN MISUNDERSTOOD

I

OF BAPTISM

THE AUGSBURG CONFESSION DOES NOT TEACH THE ABSOLUTE NECESSITY OF BAPTISM TO SALVATION

1. "THIS disease, or original fault, is truly sin, condemning and bringing eternal death now also upon all that are not born again by baptism and the Holy Spirit." Art. II, 3.

These words are substantially a repetition of the language of our Lord: John 3:5: "Except a man be born of the water and of the Spirit, he cannot enter into the kingdom of God."

Our Savior's words and the Confession mean that to everyone "born of the flesh," there is an absolute necessity of regeneration, or the new birth, of which the Holy Spirit is always the cause, and Baptism the ordinary, yet not absolutely essential means. The language, in neither case, is

meant to exclude the idea that when the ordinary
means cannot be had, the Holy Ghost may cause
the new birth in a direct or extraordinary way.

2. "Of Baptism, they teach that it is necessary
to salvation." Art. IX, 1.

That is, as instituted and commanded of God
our Savior, as an ordinary means of salvation,
which we are bound to use, yet not in such sense
of absolute necessity that salvation is in no case to
be had without it, if it cannot be obtained.

3. "They condemn the Anabaptists, who allow
not the Baptism of children, and affirm that
children are saved without Baptism." Art. IX, 3.

God's operations are usually by means; his
ordinary operations by ordinary means. When he
appoints no means to an end, it is not to be
presumed that he designs that end, or if he
demonstrably purposes a certain end, the inference
is just that he has certain means for it. Infants are
ordinarily saved by Baptism as God's ordinary
means, but God is not so bound to the means that
He cannot save them without means. The
Anabaptist doctrine was that children are not
saved by the grace of the Holy Ghost in Baptism,
even when they receive it,—but if they are saved at
all, are saved without regeneration, of which it was
assumed they had no need, or that if regenerated
they were ordinarily regenerated without any
ordinary means whatever. This doctrine our
Confession rejected, holding that infants always
required regeneration, were ordinarily saved by
Baptism as the ordinary means, and that when

deprived of it their regeneration and salvation were extraordinary; that is, special, and out of the usual order of God's arrangement. The doctrine that God has appointed no ordinary means for the salvation of infants throws doubts upon their salvation, while the doctrine of the Confession creates the strongest assurance that He who has appointed ordinary means for infant salvation, so heartily desires it, that when the ordinary means fail, He will secure it in some other way.

4. In regard to the salvation of infants dying unbaptized, the language of Luther is very explicit. In his "Christliche Bedencken," published in 1542, in reply to the anxious questions of Christian mothers, he rebukes and forbids the superstitious practice of the Roman Church, of baptizing a child not fully born—a practice based upon the idea, of the absolute necessity of Baptism, to the salvation of a child, and which would find some justification in that theory.

He directs, that those who are present, shall hold firmly to Christ's words: "Unless a man be born again, he cannot enter into the kingdom of God," and shall kneel down, and, in faith, pray that the Lord will make this (unbaptized) child, partaker in his sufferings and death, and shall *then not doubt*, that He knows full well how, according to his divine grace and pity, to fulfil that prayer.

Wherefore, since the little child (unbaptized) has, by our earnest prayer, been brought to Christ, and this prayer has been uttered in faith, what we beg, is established with God, and heard of him, and he gladly receiveth it (the child): as he himself says, Mark 10:14: "Suffer little children to come unto me, and forbid them not: for of such is the kingdom of God." Then should we hold that the little child, though it has not obtained Baptism, is not on that account lost ("das Kindlein, ob es wohl die rechte Taufe nicht erlanget, davon nicht verlohren ist)." There are other passages in Luther, on the same subject, but what we have given is sufficient.

5. This "Bedencken" of Luther's, was accompanied by an Exposition of the 29th Psalm, by Bugenhagen (Pomeranus), which Luther indorses. The main object of Bugenhagen, in the Treatise, is to give consolation in regard to unbaptized children, over against, what he styles, "the shameful error, drawn not from God's Word, but from man's dreams, that such children are lost." Bugenhagen, after teaching parents to commit to God, in prayer, their child which cannot be baptized, adds: "This shall we *assuredly believe*, that Christ receives the child, and we should not commit it to the secret judgment of God. To commit it to the secret judgment of God, is to throw to the wind, and despise the promises in regard to little children." Both Luther and Bugenhagen discuss, at large, the arguments for, and the objections against the doctrine of the salvation of unbaptized children, and demonstrate that it is no part of the faith of our Church, that Baptism is *absolutely* necessary; that is, that there are no *exceptions* nor *limitations* to the proposition that, unless a man be born again, of water or Baptism, he cannot enter the kingdom of God.

LUTHER AND BUGENHAGEN condemn those who refuse to unbaptized children, the rites of Christian burial, and who object to lay their bodies in consecrated ground, as if they were outside of the Church. "We bury them," say they, "as Christians, confessing, thereby, that we believe the strong assurance of Christ." "The bodies of these (unbaptized) children, have part in the joyous Resurrection—the Resurrection of life."

II

PERSON OF CHRIST

THE AUGSBURG CONFESSION DOES NOT TEACH THE ESSENTIAL OMNIPRESENCE OR LOCAL UBIQUITY OF THE HUMAN NATURE OF OUR LORD

"There are two natures, the Divine and human, *inseparably* joined together." Art. III, 2.

This means that the Divine and human natures are not only never separated, but are incapable of separation, either in time or space. As there is, since the incarnation, *no time at which* they have been or will be separated, so is there *no place in which* they are or will be separated. But this is not because the human nature has an *essential omnipresence*, that is, the power in and of itself to be everywhere present, but because it is rendered present in, through, and by the Divine nature, with whose person it is in unity. Nor is this personal omnipresence of our Lord's human nature a local ubiquity, but as the Divine nature is present essentially in and of itself, without extension or locality, so does it render the human nature present without extension or locality. The presence of each is equally real, and equally incomprehensible, the Divine present of itself, and the human rendered present though the Divine.

III

CONSUBSTANTIATION

THE AUGSBURG CONFESSION DOES NOT TEACH THE
DOCTRINE OF CONSUBSTANTIATION

1. "Of the Supper of the Lord they teach that the [true] body and blood of Christ are truly present." Art. X, l.

"Christ's body," says Luther, "has three modes of presence: First. The comprehensible, corporal mode, such as he used when he was on earth, local. To this mode of presence the Scripture refers, when it says Christ has left the world. Second. In another incomprehensible and spiritual mode, it can be present, illocally. Moreover, it can be present in a Divine and heavenly mode, since it is one person with God." The current error about this view of our Church is, that she holds that the body and blood of Christ are present in the first of these modes,—a view she entirely rejects. Though she denies that this presence is merely spiritual, if the word spiritual means such as is wrought by our spirit, our meditations, our faith, yet over against all carnal or local presence, she maintains that it is spiritual. "When," says the Formula of Concord, "Dr. Luther or we use this word 'spiritually,' in reference to this matter, we mean that *spiritual, supernatural, heavenly* mode, according to which

Christ is present at the Holy Supper.... By that word 'spiritually,' we design to exclude those Capernaitish imaginings of a gross and carnal presence, which, after *so many public protestations* on the part of our Churches, the Sacramentarians still try to fix on them. In this sense we say that the body and blood of Christ in the Supper is received, eaten and drunken, *spiritually*.... The *mode is spiritual.*"

2. "[Under the form of bread and wine]." Art. X, 2.

The first object of this part of the Article was to reject the Roman doctrine, Transubstantiation.

By the "form or species of bread and wine," is meant, as the Apology expresses it (X, 54), "the visible things, to wit, bread and wine." The Reformers had long before rejected and refuted the doctrine of Transubstantiation. In the Smalcald Articles (VI, 5), Luther and our Church say: "We despise the sophistic subtlety of Transubstantiation, in which they feign that the bread and wine lose their natural substance—and that the mere form and color of bread—not real bread, remain."

Another object was to reject the Roman abuse of withholding the cup from the laity; hence the Confession says "bread *and wine*"—and under the Abuses (Art. XXII), a fuller statement in regard to the Communion, in both kinds, is given.

So in the Formula of Concord, 541, 22: "We reject and condemn, with unanimous consent, the Papal Transubstantiation."

"We reject and condemn with heart and mouth, as false and full of fraud, first of all, the Popish Transubstantiation." (Formula of Concord, 670, 108.)

"It is said that the body and blood of Christ are '*under* the form of bread and wine,' and '*in* the Supper,' not to imply a local conjunction or presence, but for other and very different reasons."

"Our first reason for using the phrases, that the body of Christ is under, with, in the bread, is by them to reject the Popish Transubstantiation, and to set forth that the substance of the bread is unchanged." (Formula of Concord, 654, 35.)

The words "under" and "in," are meant to teach that "the bread which we break, and the cup we bless, are the *Communion* of the body and blood of Christ;" that is, communicate that body and blood to us,—or, in other words, we receive the body and blood, *with* the bread and wine, or "in" or "under" them as a *medium.*

By, in, with, and under the act of receiving the sacramental bread and wine truly and naturally, we receive the body and blood of Christ, substantially present, truly and supernaturally, after a heavenly and spiritual manner.

Thus also, by, in, with, and under the act of receiving the word of God truly and naturally, we receive the Holy Spirit, substantially present, truly and supernaturally, after a heavenly and spiritual manner. As the ear is the natural organ of the supernatural reception in the one case, so is the mouth in the other. As we hear the Holy Ghost in, with, and under the Word, so do we eat Christ's body in, with, and under the bread. "The reception is oral, but the mode is spiritual."

Our Confession, then, in rejecting the heresy of Transubstantiation, does not mean to substitute for it "Consubstantiation," or the doctrine of a local or physical presence of the body and blood of Christ, and a local or physical conjunction of them with the bread and wine, or a natural and carnal eating and drinking of them,—all of which errors our Church has *more fully and explicitly officially rejected* than any other part of the Christian world.

3. Testimonies of our great divines, from Luther to the present hour, without number, might be adduced to show that the Lutheran Church has never held the doctrine of Consubstantiation. In regard to LUTHER, MELANCHTHON, JONAS, CREUTZIGER, BUGENHAGEN, MENIUS, and MYCONIUS, it will not be necessary to produce any evidence from their private writings, as there is ample evidence as to their views in a great official document, prepared and signed by them. This is the ARTICLES OF THE WITTENBERG CONCORD, of 1536, in which it is declared to be sound doctrine, on the part of Bucer, and of those with whom the Concord was formed, that "they deny that any Transubstantiation takes place, and do not hold that the body and blood of Christ are locally included in the elements."

4. We will quote a few other testimonies in chronological order:

ANDREW OSIANDER (Chancellor of the University of Tubingen). (1617): "Our theologians for years long have strenuously denied, and *powerfully confuted* the doctrine of a local inclusion, or physical connection of the body and bread, or Consubstantiation. We believe in no impanation, subpanation, companation, or consubstantiation of the body of Christ, no physical or local inclusion or conjoining of bread and body, as our adversaries, in manifest calumnies, allege against us. The expressions in, with, and under are used, first, in order to proscribe the MONSTROUS DOCTRINE of TRANSUBSTANTIATION, and secondly, to assert a true presence over against the doctrine that the Lord's Supper is a mere sign."

5. MENTZER (1627): "There is no local concealment of Christ's body, or inclusion of particles of matter under the bread. Far from us be it that any believer should regard Christ's body as present in a physical or natural mode. The eating and drinking are not natural or Capernaitish, but mystical or sacramental."

6. JOHN GERHARD (1637): "On account of the *calumnies* of our adversaries, we would note that we do not believe in *impanation*, nor in CONSUBSTANTIATION, nor in any *physical* or *local* presence. Some of our writers, adopting a phrase from Cyrill, have called the presence a *bodily* one, but they use that term by no means to designate the mode of presence, but simply the object" (to show *what* is present, to wit, the body of Christ, but not *how* it is present), "nor have they at all meant by this that the body of Christ is present in a bodily and quantitative manner." "We believe in no consubstantiative presence of the body and

blood. Far from us be that figment. The heavenly thing and the earthly thing in the Lord's Supper are not present with each other, *physically and naturally.*"

7. CARPZOV (1657): "To compress into a few words what is most important in regard to this presence, we would remark: 1. That it is not finite, either physical, or local, or definite, but infinite and Divine. 2. That as there is not one mode only of Divine presence, but that presence may be *general*, or gracious, or glorious, as the scholastics distinguish it, so this presence (of the body and blood of Christ) is neither to be referred to the *general* nor the *glorious*, but to the *gracious*, so that it constitutes that special degree of this gracious presence which is styled *sacramental.* That which is supernatural is also true and real. When this presence is called *substantial* and *bodily*, those words designate *not* the MODE of presence, but the OBJECT. When the words *in, with, under*, are used, our traducers know as well as they know their own fingers, that they do NOT signify, a CONSUBSTANTIATION, local coexistence, or impanation. The charge that we hold a local inclusion, or Consubstantiation, is a calumny. The eating and drinking are not physical, but *mystical* and *sacramental.* An action is not necessarily figurative because it is not physical."

8. BAIER, J. G. (1695): "The sacramental union is neither *substantial*, nor *personal*, nor *local.* Hence it is manifest that *impanation* and *Consubstantiation*, which are charged upon Lutherans by enemies, are utterly excluded. There is no sensible or natural

eating of the body of Christ. Alike the presence and the eating and drinking of the body and blood of Christ are insensible, supernatural, unknown to the human mind, and incomprehensible. As to the MODE in which the body and blood of Christ are present and received in the Supper, we may acknowledge our *ignorance*, while we firmly hold to the *fact*." The same distinguished writer published a dissertation on "Impanation and Consubstantiation," which is entirely devoted to the vindication of our Church from the charge of holding these errors.

9. LEIBNITZ (d. 1716), distinguished as a profound theological thinker, as well as a philosopher of the highest order, says: "Those who receive the Evangelical (Lutheran) faith by no means approve the doctrine of CONSUBSTANTIATION, or of impanation, nor can any one impute it to them, unless from a misunderstanding of what they hold."

10. BUDDEUS (1728): "All who understand the doctrines of our Church know that with our WHOLE SOUL WE ABHOR THE DOCTRINE OF CONSUBSTANTIATION AND OF A GROSS UBIQUITY OF THE FLESH OF CHRIST. They are greatly mistaken who suppose the doctrine of impanation to be the doctrine of Luther and of our Church. The doctrine of impanation, if we distinguish it from that of assumption, can mean nothing else than a local inclusion of the body of Christ in the bread. To admit such a doctrine would be to *admit the grossest absurdities*: they, therefore, who impute it to our Church, prove *only their ignorance* of our

doctrine. In *either sense* in which the word CONSUBSTANTIATION can be taken, the doctrine cannot, *in any respect*, be attributed to our Church; it was always far from the mind of our Church. The sacramental union is one which reason cannot comprehend, and the taking, eating, and drinking, are done in sublime mystery."

11. COTTA (1779) makes the following remarks upon the different theories of sacramental union:

"By IMPANATION, is meant a *local inclusion* of the body and blood in the bread and wine. Gerhard has rightly noted that the theologians of our Church utterly abhor this error. The particles in, with, under, are not used to express a local inclusion. As our theologians reject impanation, so also they reject the doctrine of CONSUBSTANTIATION. This word is taken in two senses. It denotes sometimes a *local conjunction* of two bodies, sometimes a *commingling* or *coalescence* into one substance or mass. But in *neither sense* can that MONSTROUS DOGMA of CONSUBSTANTIATION be attributed to our Church, for Lutherans believe neither in a local conjunction, nor commixture of bread and Christ's body, nor of wine and Christ's blood."

12. Many of the greatest divines of other Churches have acknowledged the libelous character of the charge that the Lutheran Church holds the doctrine of CONSUBSTANTIATION; and many of the deepest thinkers, not of our Communion, have approached very closely to its doctrine, or have accepted it unreservedly.

IV

AURICULAR CONFESSION

THE AUGSBURG CONFESSION REJECTS AURICULAR
CONFESSION, AND DOES NOT TEACH THE NECESSITY OF
PRIVATE CONFESSION

1. "Enumeration of all offences is not necessary in Confession. For it is impossible; according to the Psalm: 'Who can understand his errors?' " Art. XI, 1, 2; XXV, 7–12.

In this, Auricular Confession is rejected.

"Confession is of human right only [is not commanded in Scripture, but has been instituted by the Church]." Art. XXV, 12.

In this is denied that private Confession is necessary.

2. "Concerning Confession, they teach that private absolution be retained in the Church." Art. XI, 1. "Confession is not abolished in our Churches." Art. XXV, 1. "On account of the very great benefit of absolution, as well as for other uses to the conscience, Confession is retained among us." Do., 13.

The question is sometimes put, How can this eleventh Article be harmonized with the position of those who consider all the doctrinal Articles of the Augsburg Confession as Articles of Faith, and therefore fundamental, and who yet do not practice "private Confession?" This is a fair question, if honestly put, and deserves a frank reply.

The facts bearing upon the question may be thus arranged:

1. The first XXI Articles of the Augsburg Confession are styled in the general title "Principal Articles of Faith," or, as in the German, "Articles of Faith and Doctrine." At the end of these it is declared: "This is almost a summary of *doctrine* among us, in which it can be perceived that there is *nothing* which is discrepant with the *Scriptures.* In the Articles of Faith there is *nothing* taught in our Churches contrary to the *Holy Scriptures*, or to the Universal Christian Church."

2. For it was then, as ever, an axiom of our Church, that "the *Word of God* shall make Articles of Faith, and none other besides, no, not an angel even." The Church Catholic, or the Holy Christian Church Universal, cannot make Articles of Faith; she can only confess them as her own.

3. An Article of Faith is, therefore, something which rests on Divine authority; is absolute in its claim on our acceptance, and is not controlled in any way by the liberty of the Church.

4. If, therefore, under the XXI "Articles of Faith," there were found something which the Confessors, in so many terms, in the Confession itself, declare to be no Article of Faith, but a matter of Church freedom, subject to the control of the various parts of the Church, in different ages and in different regions in the same age, the inference would be a very just one, that such a statement of usage found its way into a doctrinal article simply because of its natural connection with some Article of Faith, though not an essential part of it. If, therefore, our Confessors had, among the Articles

of Faith, expressed a desire to retain for *their own time* "private Confession," because, although of human origin, it was useful, the inference would not be a just one, that we were to make an Article of Faith out of that which they avowed to be a matter of Christian liberty, and which they therefore considered subject to such change, as the Church, in different eras, lands or circumstances, might see fit to make.

The principle of the Lutheran Church on this point is thus defined in the Formula of Concord:

"Ceremonies or ecclesiastical rites [Church usages], which are neither commanded nor forbidden in God's Word, but which are instituted alone for the sake of comeliness or good order, are not in themselves, or *per se*, Divine worship, or a part of it."

"The Church of God, of every part of the world, and of every time, according as her own occasion demands, has power to change such ceremonies, in such a way as she may judge most useful and edifying to the Church of God."

"No Church should condemn another, because it has fewer or more outward ceremonies not commanded by God, provided that in doctrine and all its articles, and in the true use of the Sacraments, there be unity between them."

The principle here involved is, therefore, very simple. When we subscribe a Confession *ex animo*, we receive it according to the mind and intent of its framers. What they set forth as Articles of Faith we receive as such, declaring their faith to be our faith; what they set forth as argument, we consider as argument, and weigh it as such; what they set forth avowedly as personal preference, we consider as such, and look upon our Christian liberty as not bound authoritatively by theirs. The unity of the Church is a unity of faith,—they only are really one who have one faith: but they may sustain that faith by different arguments. They are one in the reception of the Sacraments in all their divinely-appointed essentials, but they may approve of different usages in the confessedly human arrangements connected with them.

If it can be shown that our Confessors declared private Confession to be no matter of faith, although they preferred to use it, as good, though human, their preference has no binding power for us. In everything confessedly subject to Christian freedom, the Evangelical Lutheran Church in America has the same liberty of choice as our Church has in any other part of the world; and in this sphere, the Lutheran Church of the Nineteenth Century has the same inalienable rights as the Church of the Sixteenth Century. Our Church, in this land, and at this time, has full power, on the general New Testament principles of Evangelical Lutheranism, to adapt herself, by new human usages, not contrary to the spirit of God's Word, to her present position; and however widely they may differ from those of our fathers, we are none the less, their true, spiritual children, while we are one with them in faith. The Lutheran Church is a free Church. She is the freest of all Churches in true freedom. She acknowledges no *authority* but that of her Lord, but that is supreme. And because of her true freedom, and her repudiation of all authority but *His*, she stands inflexibly by her

Confession of His truth; for if that Confession be lax, she is at the mercy of men, of whims, of errorists, of the spirit of the hour, of schism: she ceases to utter her testimony as a Church; no one can tell where she stands; she has as many faiths, or as many unbeliefs, as may be invented for her; she has no voice for her children; she becomes a Babel. If, therefore, it shall be shown that "private Confession" was considered as an Article of Faith by our Church, we cannot, consistently, with a pretense to be in unity with her, reject it.

5. The Augsburg Confession is matchless in its accuracy. He who will study it for years, closely comparing it with God's Word, and with the History of Doctrines, will find it hard to restrain his admiration within the bounds of cold sobriety. It never puts in a word without a reason, it *never leaves out, without reason, a word* that might be anticipated.

This Eleventh Article beautifully illustrates the exquisite caution and care with which every word was weighed, and how exactly what was meant to be expressed, was expressed, and how exactly what was meant to, be omitted, was omitted.

a. Mark that not one word is said about "*private* Confession." The word is not there. It is not said that "private *Confession*" nor any other Confession is to be retained, and yet so natural would it be to say something about it, that the Article, superficially read, seems to lack finish, if not perfect coherence, for want of such a mention. Why was this? Because here are the "principal Articles of *faith*," and *Confession* was no Article of Faith, because, as the IVth Article on Abuses says:

"Confession is not commanded in the Scriptures, but was instituted by the Church." This, then, is our answer as regards "private *Confession*," that the Augsburg Confession not only does not make it an Article of Faith, but denies it to be such, first negatively, in the Eleventh Article, where it *must* have been mentioned, had they considered it as such, and, secondly, positively in the IVth Article on Abuses, where the Confession declares, in positive terms, that Confession, in any form, is not an Article of Faith, but a usage of the Church, retained by our Churches at that time because they found it useful.

b. While the doctrinal Articles of the Confession do not exhibit "private Confession," nor any other, as an Article of Faith, yet in view of the fact, that a perfectly free, personal interview between the pastor and the individual member of his flock was retained by the Churches in their Christian freedom, it does set forth as an Article of Faith, that Auricular Confession, practiced in the Church of Rome, requiring the mention of an offence as a preliminary to its absolution, is contrary to Holy Scripture.

c. The Eleventh Article teaches that "*private absolution* is to be retained in the Churches."

On this it is worthy of notice:

1. That in both the phrases "*private* Confession," and "*private* absolution," the word "private" is used *not* in the sense of "sequestered from company; secret," but in the sense of "individual, not general, separate." That *incidentally*, either of them might be private in the former sense, and that, especially, anything like a

free confession should be made ordinarily in privacy, and was so made, is true; but in neither case is this sort of privacy essential to the idea of the word. A man may make a "private confession" in the presence of others, and does so, when, for himself, he confesses his own sins. A man receives "private absolution," no matter how many may be present, when to himself individually, the Divine promise is set forth. Hence "private confession" and "private absolution" are separable. "Private absolution" may be given when there has been no Confession at all, or where the Confession is general. This very separation takes place in the usage of the Danish Churches. In preparing for the Lord's Supper, there is a *general Confession* of Sins. The communicants then kneeling around the altar together, the minister lays his hand on each person, successively, and pronounces a *private* or individual *Absolution.* In a word, both Confession and Absolution, which are private in one sense, may be public in another.

2. Private Confession and private Absolution are not only distinct and separable, but they belong to different spheres. Private Confession is human: it is a thing which the Church is at liberty to have or not have, as in any particular country or time she sees best; its chief value, when it is used aright, is, that it enables a faithful pastor to make his instruction specific in its adaptation to the wants of the individual; and, most of all, because it prepares the mind for Scriptural and Evangelical views of the real character and value of Absolution. "Confession is retained among us on account of the *very great benefit* of absolution

[which is the main thing therein], as well as for other uses to the conscience." It was at the Confessional Luther began his work as a Reformer,—and private Confession was the great bulwark against Auricular Confession, and all the other false doctrines and practices of the time. "It was specially designed," says Luther, in the Smalcald Articles, "for the young, that they might be conversed with, examined, and instructed in the teaching of Christ." The enumeration of sins was free,—it was, in a word, essentially no more than an interview between pastor and communicant, a blessed privilege, not a legal exaction.

The private Confession which our Church has used has been most happy in its working; in the hands of faithful men it has done more than all other human arrangements for maintaining a living piety, and pure discipline in the Church; even those not of our Church, as for example Zwingli and Calvin, have approved of it; the later Helvetic Confession and the Heidelberg Catechism leave it free; the Church of England expressly provided for it at first, and Alting says: "It is an atrocious calumny that the Calvinistic Churches neglect the practice of private Confession and absolution."

Earnest men of our own time, not only of a thoroughly churchly spirit, but even those who regard private Confession solely in the light of its personal benefits, have desired to see it restored. Tholuck, for example, mourning that private Confession had fallen, enumerating the loss of it as among the "injuries and wounds of the Church," appeals to the students of theology before whom he preached: "Ye that are to be the ministers of the Word in time to come, regard it as your vocation, to heal these wounds of our Church, and to restore to it *private Confession*, not Auricular Confession, which this Article rejects."‖

3. Absolution itself, that is, "God's Word which forgives sin," is of Divine appointment. "The commission and power of the keys" is His, and to that forgiving Word of His, which he commands his ministers to utter, faith is to listen no less than if "God's voice sounded out of heaven." This word of Absolution is the Gospel itself, offering grace to all who hear it, and actually conferring forgiveness on all who receive it in faith. But this Absolution is not only to be offered to men in the aggregate, but to each and every sin-burdened soul, as occasion offers; and whenever, and in whatever outward mode it is then offered, it is a "private Absolution." In this, its essence, it abides in the Church.

When any minister of Christ offers to the true, individual penitent, the Divine promise of forgiveness for Christ's sake, he offers "private Absolution." With all the mutilations of unbelief, and all the deviations from the beautiful and fitting modes in which the Office of the Keys was administered in our Church in the era of the Reformation, the faithful pastor, who is true to the spirit of the Gospel, does not utterly lose the essence in the loss of the form, and in such hands, it may still be said, that "private Absolution is retained in our Churches." The whole Pastoral work is, indeed, but an extension of this idea in its true conception.

V

THE MASS

THE AUGSBURG CONFESSION DOES NOT COUNTENANCE
THE ROMAN MASS NOR ITS CEREMONIES, BUT REJECTS
AND CONDEMNS BOTH

1. "Our Churches are wrongfully accused to have abolished the Mass." Art. XXIV, 1.

It is only necessary to read the Article through to see that the Confession sets forth the Mass in its original and proper sense, to note the celebration of the Lord's Supper, and contrasts it with the Roman Mass, or corruption of that Supper into a sacrifice. The ceremonies retained are those which are really ceremonies appropriate to the original idea of the Mass, that is, to the celebration of the Lord's Supper, to wit, the reading of God's Word, prayers, psalms, hymns, and thanksgivings.

VI

THE SABBATH AND THE LORD'S DAY

THE AUGSBURG CONFESSION DOES NOT DENY THE
OBLIGATION OF KEEPING THE LORD'S DAY

1. "They that think that the *observation* of the Lord's Day was appointed by the authority of the Church, instead of the Sabbath, *as necessary*, are greatly deceived." Art. XXVIII, 58.

The emphasis is on the words *"observation"* and "necessary."

The Confessors maintained that the *Jewish Sabbath* is abrogated, but that so far as its ends and obligations were original and generic they are unchangeable, and that to meet these ends and obligations the Christian Church, through the Apostles, had appointed the first day of the week, or Lord's Day. In what they here say they mean to confute two Roman errors. The first was that of the "*observation*" of days, that is, of *such* a keeping as was Judaizing in its spirit, and opposed to the grace of the Gospel, such as St. Paul expressly condemned when he says: "Ye *observe* days.... I am afraid lest I have bestowed labor upon you in vain." Galat. 4:10. Secondly, the idea that such outward observation was in itself meritoriously *necessary* to salvation. This the Confession denied, and shows that there is a necessity for the Lord's Day, but not of the kind Roman Catholicism had invented.

2. A systematic statement of the predominant doctrine of the Sabbath *involved* in the views of the greatest writers of our Church, may be presented in the following propositions:

1. The law that one day in seven shall be set apart for the service of God, has existed by Divine command, from the foundation of the world, and its obligation is a part of the original law of nature.

2. The command was repeated in the Decalogue and in the Mosaic law, with specific ceremonial characteristics adapting it to the Jewish nation.

3. The law itself, generically considered, is of perpetual and universal obligation; its specific ceremonial characteristics pertain only to the Jews.

4. The law itself has never been abrogated; the specific ceremonial characteristics have been.

5. To keep one day in seven holy to God, to abstain from all that may conflict with its sanctification, is generic, not specific; moral, not ceremonial.

6. The obligation to keep holy the seventh day, or Saturday, is ceremonial, and not binding on Christians.

7. The resurrection of Christ, his successive appearings, the Pentecostal effusion of his Spirit, on the first day of the week, together with the example of the Apostles, and of the Apostolic Church, have shown to the Church what day in the seven may, under the New Dispensation, most fitly be kept holy, and have led to the substitution of the first day of the week for the seventh, as the Christian Sabbath.

8. To keep holy the first day of the week, to consecrate it to God, and to this end to abstain upon it from all works except those of necessity, mercy, and the service of God, is obligatory on all men.

No Church can show a purer record than the Lutheran Church, on this very question of sound doctrine in regard to the moral and Divine obligation to consecrate one day in every seven to God, and to repose from toil. The greatest leaders of theology in our Church, considered a denial of the Divine obligation to keep one day in seven as *Socinian.* The Sabbatarians, harmonizing with the Jews, considered even the determinative part of the fourth command as perpetual, and contended that Saturday should be kept. Our fathers rejected this error. The Anabaptists and Socinians contended that no part of the fourth command is of Divine obligation—that all is ceremonial. Our fathers rejected this error, and rested on this point as in others, on the truth removed from each extreme— that the generic Sabbath is primitive and has never been abrogated—that only what is ceremonial in the Jewish Sabbath is abrogated—that the Christian Sabbath is a glorious bond of the sovereignty of God in the law, and of the freedom of the Church under the Gospel; *Divine in its generic origin and obligation, and apostolic in its specific determination.*

In addition to the works already cited, the English reader will find matter of value on the history or meaning of the Augsburg Confession in: "The Life of Melanchthon," by C. F. Ledderhose, translated by Rev. G. F. Krotel, D.D., 1855; "A Plea for the Augsburg Confession" (1856), and "Lutheranism in America" (1857), by W. J. Mann, D.D.; Dr. C. F. Schaeffer's brief, but valuable notes on the Confession; and "Digest of Christian Doctrine," by J. A. Seiss, D.D., 1857.